GYMNASTICS FOUNDATIONS

D1133692

Author Keith Russell

Layout Gene Schembri

Art Georges McKail

Project Management Beverley Dickinson

Copyright

GYMNASTICS FOUNDATIONS

Author: Keith Russell

Published in 2008 by Ruschkin Publishing
1st edition
Address: Box 363, RPO University
          Saskatoon, SK S7N 4J8
          Canada

Published in 2010 by Ruschkin Publishing
2nd edition

Printed in Canada

ISBN 978-0-920611-45-6

Acknowledgements

EXPERT GROUP

Elisabeth Bureaud, Gymnastics Canada
Cathy Haines, Sport Consultant
Doug Hillis, University of Saskatchewan
Marta Kroupa, Rhythmic Gymnastics, Master Course Conductor
Pat Leith, Theory Learning Facilitator
Heather McManus, Trampoline Gymnastics, Master Course Conductor

PHOTO CREDITS

Grace Chiu/GraceClick
Hardy Fink
Karl Wharton
F.I.G. Book: "100 Years of the International Gymnastics Federation 1881 - 1991"

Gymnastic Canada would like to thank, in particular, Gymnastics Saskatchewan, the Alberta Gymnastics Federation, Gymnastics British Columbia, and Gymnastics Ontario, for their support and collaboration in the piloting of this course and all the coaches who participated in the pilot courses.

The National Coaching Certification Program is a collaborative program of the Government of Canada, provincial/territorial governments, national/provincial/territorial sport federations, and the Coaching Association of Canada.

Partners in Coach Education

The programs of this organization are funded in part by Sport Canada.

Canadian Heritage
Patrimoine canadien
Sport Canada

Contents

QUESTION SECTION

1

So You Want to be a Coach

GYMnastics
nastique
CANADA

Coaching
Association
of Canada

National
Coaching
Certification
Program

SO YOU WANT TO BE A COACH

Welcome to the introductory course on Coach Education offered by Gymnastics Canada (GCG). This General Foundations Course and text introduces you to several sports and activities that are collectively called GYMNASTICS.

After completing this course you will then be eligible to enrol in the Specific Foundations Courses, each of which focuses on one gymnastics sport (also called disciplines by the International Gymnastics Federation - FIG).

Q | Complete   Q 1 & 2

The Many Meanings of 'Coach'

Of course the answer to each of the 5 questions is YES.

In most vocations and professions there are clearly delineated descriptors for persons with different training. Take for example:

Dental Receptionist, Dental Hygienist, Dental Technician, Dental Assistant, Denturist, Dentist, Orthodontist.

Exercise Therapist, Physical Therapist, Occupational Therapist, Massage Therapist, Aroma Therapist, Athletic Therapist.

Coaches work in many different contexts, and have many different levels of training but they are all referred to as "coaches".

The National Coaching Certification Program (NCCP) in Canada is being updated to rectify this confusion.

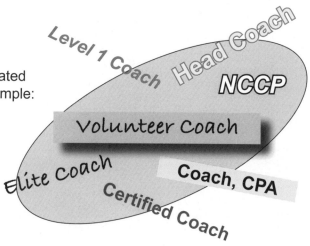

Level 1 Coach   Head Coach   NCCP   Volunteer Coach   Elite Coach   Coach, CPA   Certified Coach

OVERVIEW OF NATIONAL COACHING CERTIFICATION PROGRAM

The NCCP

The structure of the NCCP is designed to take into account the different types of coaches that contribute to the Canadian sport system, and the environment or context in which they coach.

The structure of the NCCP is, therefore, based on Coaching Streams and on specific Coaching Contexts within each Stream. Three distinct Coaching Streams have been identified: Community Sport, Competition, and Instruction.

Each national sport organization has the responsibility to determine the coaching streams and contexts that apply to its coach development system.

Gymnastics Canada has chosen to train coaches in the Community Sport and Competitive streams. The Foundations courses are designed for coaches in the initiation context of Community Sport.

NCCP - 3 Streams	
①	Community Sport
②	Competition
③	Instruction

National Coaching Certification Program

NCCP PROGRAM OVERVIEW

Thy National Coaching Certification Program (NCCP) is a coach training and certification program for all coaches in more than 60 sports. The NCCP is moving towards a competency – based approach where coaches are:

- Trained in NCCP outcomes relevant to the participants that they are coaching
- Evaluated by demonstrating coaching outcomes to a specified standard

The core competencies of coaching are valuing, interacting, leading, problem-solving, and critical thinking. These competencies will be woven through all NCCP training and evaluation activities.

Who am I coaching?

The new structure of the NCCP is based on the participants' needs, which are identified within streams and contexts.

Community Sport stream
Initiation CSp-Init
Ongoing participation CSp-Ong

Competition stream
Introduction Comp-Int
Development Comp-Dev
High performance Comp-HP

Instruction stream
Beginners Inst-Beg
Intermediate performers Inst-Imd
Advanced performers Inst-Adv

Initiation context
Participants of all ages are encouraged to participate in the sport and introduced to sport basics in a fun, safe, and self-esteem building environment regardless of their ability.

Ongoing participation context
Participants of all ages are encouraged to continue participating in the sport for fun, fitness, skill development, and social interaction.

Introduction context
Children and/or adolescents are taught basic sport skills and athletic abilities in a fun and safe environment and are typically prepared for local and/or regional level competitions.

Development context
Adolescents and young adults are coached to refine basic sport skills, to develop more advanced skills and tactics, and are generally prepared for performance at provincial and/or national level competitions.

High performance context
Young adults are coached to refine advanced skills and tactics and are typically prepared for performance at national and international level competitions.

Beginners context
Participants of all ages, with little or no sport experience, are taught basic sport skills.

Intermediate performers context
Participants, who already have some experience and proficiency in the sport, are taught to refine basic skills and introduced to more complex techniques.

Advanced performers context
Participants who are experienced and already proficient in the sport are taught to refine advanced skills and techniques.

What do I need to be able to do?

Within each context, coaching outcomes are defined by the National Sport Organizations (NSOs) that clearly outline what you must be able to do in order to meet the needs of participants in that context. Contact your NSO to find out which context is relevant to you and what you need to do to achieve accreditation.

Coaching Outcomes

- Make Ethical Decisions
- Provide Support to Athletes in Training
- Plan a Practice
- Support the Competitive Experience
- Analyze Performance
- Design a Sport Program
- Manage a Program
- Sport-specific Outcomes (as determined by the Sport)

How do I achieve accreditation?

Coaches can receive three types of accreditation in any of the above contexts:

 In Training
Coach needs to be trained in additional outcomes.

✓ **Trained**
Coach has completed training in designated outcomes.

✓ **Certified**
Coach has been evaluated in designated outcomes and has acknowledged the NCCP Code of Conduct.

Coaching Association of Canada

For more information about the NCCP go to www.coach.ca

The National Coaching Certification Program is a collaborative program of the Government of Canada, provincial/territorial governments, national/provincial/territorial sport organizations, and the Coaching Association of Canada.

WHO WILL YOU COACH?

You will, for the most part, be working with children, pre-adolescents or adolescents. You will teach basic skills and help the participants improve their general fitness level.

Specialization is not a priority at this stage, rather it is more important for participants to enjoy movement.

Children

Pre-Adolescents

Adolescents

DELIVERY OPTIONS

The NCCP provides choices to sports in the delivery of the NCCP theoretical content. It can be delivered in a Multi-Sports setting where coaches from many sports are enrolled in the same course, or it can be delivered in a Sports-Specific setting. GCG has chosen the Sports-Specific delivery system whereby all the gymnastics coaches will be educated in a gymnastics-specific setting.

YOUR JOURNEY TO CERTIFICATION

NCCP Terminology

Your coaching status will change as you progress through the NCCP as follows:

1. **Coach-in-Training** - you are taking coaching courses but have not yet completed all the requirements.

2. **Trained coach** - you have completed the training requirements but have not yet been evaluated for certification.

3. **Certified coach** - you have shown competencies in a specific coaching context by having completed the evaluation.

in training …

trained …

certified …

Assessment Outcomes

The "outcomes" of this education and training will be your successful demonstration that:

• You have acquired the knowledge

• You can develop, teach and evaluate a gymnastics lesson that is safe and age and level appropriate.

Requirements for Certification

The table below provides an overview of the requirements for Certification outlining the courses, practical requirements and evaluation.

COURSES for CERTIFICATION

First course: Foundations - Technical
- 15 hour course
- Focus: Fun, Fitness and Fundamental Movement Patterns

Second course: Foundations - Theory
- 8 hour course
- Focus: Planning a lesson, Making ethical decisions

Third course: Foundations - Sport Specific
- 8 hour course
- Expands on the first two courses but in specific contexts (Active Start, Aerobic, Artistic, Rhythmic and Trampoline).

Practical

You will be guided in your practical application via a workbook that will be completed between the first 2 courses and you will continue in your practical competency building after the third course and leading up to your practical evaluation.

coach this ...

Evaluation

You will be evaluated on your understanding of the theoretical knowledge in tests and assignments during and after the courses. Your competency in the practical outcomes will be evaluated both during the courses, and finally by an evaluator who will review your coaching portfolio and observe you in a coaching environment after you have met the *training* requirements.

Complete Q16, 17 & 18 now

...ions like this appear throughout the book and are part of the evaluation.

THREE REPEATING COMPETENCY BUILDERS

In this first Gymnastics Foundations - Technical course we will reinforce your education and training program via three repeating Competency Builders, which will guide you in becoming competent in the "outcomes" on which you will be evaluated.

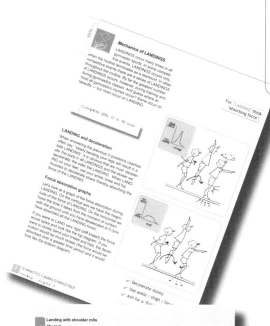

Competency Builder #1 – Knowledge (Know this)

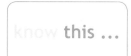

You will study theoretical material in a variety of ways such as lectures, questions, partner and group discussions. This theoretical knowledge will help you understand questions such as:

- WHY specific conditioning methods are used?
- WHY specific teaching methods are used?
- HOW biomechanical knowledge can improve technical decisions?
- WHAT are the safest ways to absorb forces on landings?

You will have many self-tests, discussions and practical exercises to assist you in applying this theoretical knowledge.

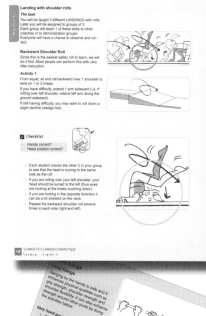

Competency Builder #2 – Experiencing (Try this)

You will be given regular opportunities to try various practical applications that illustrate the theoretical material and also refine your performance competencies in selected gymnastics activities that you will be coaching.

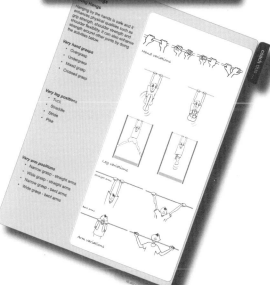

Competency Builder #3 – Coaching (Coach this)

You will regularly communicate with, and coach, other participants. At first you will observe and give feedback to a partner, but as the course progresses this will expand so that you will be coaching groups of 3, 4, and more.

You will also be given the opportunity to coach the entire course group. There will be many opportunities to receive feedback and to improve your coaching competencies.

Educational Philosophy

Fun

Fitness

FUNdamentals

OUR EDUCATIONAL PHILOSOPHY

FOCUS YOUR LEARNING

In order to be consistent from chapter to chapter and from course to course, we need a consistent Educational Philosophy that will 'focus' all of your learning experiences. The following Educational Philosophy was formulated for the first CGF Gymnastics NCCP manual and has been incorporated into all subsequent editions.

This philosophy is encapsulated with 3Fs, with each 'F' standing for a key part of the overall philosophy. Gymnastics coach education programs aim to prepare coaches and teachers who will deliver programs that ensure:

1.   Participants have FUN
2.   Participants gain FITNESS
3.   Participants acquire good FUNDAMENTALS

Participants should have FUN in gymnastics classes.

FUN

FUN

It goes without saying, if participants do not enjoy (have FUN in) gymnastics classes, they will not continue to participate.

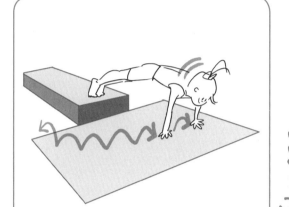

Fitness

FITNESS

Similarly, if people participate but do not have good levels of FITNESS they will not be able to correctly and easily learn gymnastics fundamentals.

FUNdamentals

FUNDAMENTALS

If they do not learn good FUNDAMENTALS, then participants are very limited in how far they can advance in any gymnastics sports.

A Guide for the Course

Throughout this course we will refer back to this Educational Philosophy and, hopefully, it will guide you after the course.

In the next chapter we take a closer look at the theoretical and practical aspects of our first philosophical goal:

Participants should have FUN in gymnastics classes.

3

Fun

FUN

FITNESS

FUNdamentals

FUN

The springing, swinging, rolling, climbing, leaping, and other activities that occur in gymnastics classes should be inherently enjoyable for participants, but we often put up barriers to participants having fun.

 Complete Q3

In the following section you will learn 3 general principles on how to make gymnastics classes FUN, and you will then experience and coach these principles.

FUN PRINCIPLE #1

Participants must be ACTIVE most of the time

There is little 'fun' in waiting in line, or watching the instructor assist one participant at a time, or playing a game that has only a few active participants while the others watch. Participants come to gymnastics classes to be active and active participants are much more likely to be having fun.

There are many ways to increase (or decrease) activity in gymnastics gyms. In the Teaching and Learning Chapter we will discuss many common practices that cause inactivity.

FUN PRINCIPLE #2

Children must be SUCCESSFUL most of the time

Children must succeed frequently in order to enjoy an activity. There are many ways to simplify skills and play games that give participants many little successes. Their enthusiasm, their self esteem, their confidence and their enjoyment are all linked to how much success they achieve in gymnastics classes.

With a partner, list 3 ways to ensure many little successes occur in gym classes, then compare your answers with other groups.

FUN PRINCIPLE #3

Children must PLAY most of the time

Complete Q4 & 5

Play is a little difficult to define. It means participants should feel exhilarated in what they are doing, they should have time to explore, they should have an opportunity to interact with other participants.

Play can, of course, be guided or focused so that some goal is achieved. In the English language we use the verb 'to play' in the context of team sports but not in the context of individual sports.

We 'play' basketball, soccer, hockey, etc. but we seldom say 'let's play gymnastics' or 'let's play figure skating' or 'play diving'. Yet that is exactly what we want participants to do — 'play' gymnastics.

Just as there are many ways to infuse our classes with playfulness, there are also many ways to do the opposite. We can overemphasize drills, orderliness, line-ups, strict adherence to schedule and to systematic physical preparation.

Competitive coaches and young coaches who are still in competitive training or recently retired from competitive training, can easily bring the work ethic of that environment into the community sport setting. This can be problematic.

Games and FUN

When we incorporate games into our gymnastics classes we encourage play. We can also design games that enhance FITNESS and FUNDAMENTALS as well.

The following is a brief introduction to the successful use of GAMES for the purpose of fostering "PLAYING gymnastics".

There are 8 guidelines for you to understand, experience and practise coaching.

> '*Play can be focused to achieve a specific goal.*'

Note

'PLAY' can be sufficiently demanding to enhance the gymnast's physicality.

Skill learning can be 'playful'.

We want participants to have FUN, and play is an important ingredient, but we also want them to become FIT and to learn FUNDAMENTALS.

PLAY IS THE MEANS, NOT THE PRIMARY GOAL

PLAY GUIDELINE #1
Safe Running in a Gymnastics Gym

1. Stop signal

At the very beginning we need to establish some ground rules for running safely in a gymnastics gym. It is important to 'sensitize' participants early in their gymnastics training (and often thereafter) about running safely.

2. Safe running tips

- Establish a STOP SIGNAL that you will use to call the group to a quick STOP.
- You could use a whistle or a loud call, but just as effective and less harsh is a signal such as raising your arm overhead.
- On this signal all participants must stop instantly.
- Practise this Stop Signal many times.
- Other signals are: 'look sharp', 'all hands on deck', 'freeze'.

3. Running and walking - games preparation

- Next, have all gymnasts run in a circle in the same direction around the free space (they will almost always do this counter clockwise).
- This is a very safe way to have participants run and is common practice for preschool participants. It is, however, limiting and not conducive to playing games.
- Now have gymnasts walk RANDOMLY around the free area such that they DO NOT TOUCH anyone else.
- Repeat with very slow RANDOM running.

Safety
Emphasize that they should keep their 'heads up' and eyes alert for other runners. They should anticipate when they would cross paths with another runner and avoid making contact. Emphasize NO CONTACT, HEADS UP, ANTICIPATE OTHERS.

4. Increase traffic by reducing floor space

Tell gymnasts 'they must not run behind you' while they do slow RANDOM running. You then walk from 1 corner of the running area, with your arms outstretched sideways, so that you are progressively restricting the size of the running area and forcing runners into a smaller and smaller area.

5. Play 'Communities'

Play a simple game such as COMMUNITIES in which the group is RANDOM RUNNING and when the coach calls out a number, they quickly sit in groups of THAT number.

Call 2 and they sit in 2's and get to know names of each other, call 4 and they sit in groups of 4, etc.

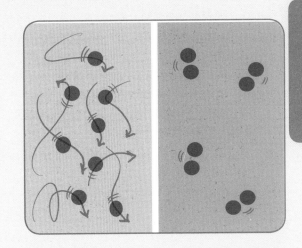

6. Partner tag

- Begin by playing COMMUNITIES to divide group into pairs.
- Have each pair of gymnasts split so they are on opposite sides of the playing area.
- Choose 1 side to be the chasers and explain that the object of the game is TO AVOID TOUCHING ANYBODY EXCEPT THEIR PARTNER.
- Then explain that the 2nd object of the game is to tag their partner, who then counts to 10 (or does 10 tuck jumps or 3 push-ups etc.) before becoming the chaser. DO NOT PLAY THIS GAME RUNNING.

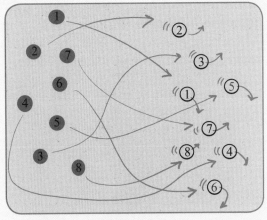

Safety

These above exercises for sensitizing participants to safe running should be practised regularly so you can safely play games (which are a key component in ensuring that participants have FUN in gymnastics classes).

7. Add geometric shapes

You can further increase their sensitivity to running safely in a confined area by having them run in different geometrical patterns while maintaining their vigilance. Have them run:

- In small circles, in large circles
- In small triangles, in large triangles
- In small squares, in large squares
- While writing their names in very large letters
- While writing Mississippi in large letters, then make 4 springs back to dot the i's.

Triangles

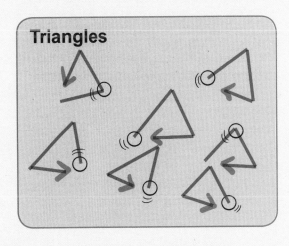

PLAY GUIDELINE #2

All participants should be ACTIVE in the game – ALL OF THE TIME

- Select games or modify games so that all participants are playing all the time.
- Avoid games in which participants are progressively eliminated.
- Avoid games that have many participants waiting for their turn.

Reasons for Inactivity

With a partner list other play activities that result in some participants being inactive:

....

....

....

....

....

PLAY GUIDELINE #3

Play COOPERATIVE as well as COMPETITIVE games

Competitive Games

There are many excellent competitive games where partners compete with one another. Wisely chosen, or creatively designed, these games can be great motivators for participants to engage in strenuous physical activity (without realizing they are actually doing conditioning exercises).

You must, of course, size-match and maturity-match the competitors in competitive activities.

Cooperative Games

There are also many co-operative activities for partners (and groups) that also provide incentive for participants to push their physical limits.

Following is a selection of competitive and co-operative games for you to begin collecting.

You will be instructed on the first few and then you will be expected to introduce several activities to your group of coaches.

A. COMPETITIVE PARTNER ACTIVITIES

1. Knee slapping

- Try to slap your partner on the knees with your hand while you block your partner from doing the same to you.

- Begin in a stationary position but later allow gymnasts to move freely so they can lunge or retreat.

2. Toe touching with toes

- Try to touch your partner's feet with your feet while avoiding your partner doing it to you.

- DO NOT stomp or kick. Just gentle toe touching.

3. Toe touching with hands

- Try to touch partner's feet with your hands while avoiding your partner doing it to you.
- BE CAREFUL not to bump heads if you both reach for each other's feet at the same time.

A. COMPETITIVE PARTNER ACTIVITY

In groups of 5, each coach will present 1 of the following activities:

1. Into the tower

- Pull partner into tower of cubes
- Partners grasp right hands over cubes
- Each tries to pull partner into cubes

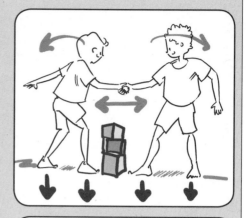

2. Into a hoop

- Pull partner into hoop
- Partners grasp right hands over hula-hoop
- Each tries to pull partner into hoop

3. Danish wrestling A

- Partners face each other, standing legs astride, holding right hands
- Without moving either foot, try to pull partner off balance
- Repeat with the left hands joined

4. Danish wrestling B

- Partners face each other, standing legs astride, holding right hands
- As above, but partners can now move their back foot to maintain balance
- Repeat with the left hands joined

5. Danish wrestling C

- Partners face each other, standing legs astride, NOT holding hands
- With either hand, push partner off balance
- No grabbing, only pushing
- Score points when either of partner's feet moves

List your activities

Additional 'Competitive Partner Activities' generated from the group.

List

B. COOPERATIVE PARTNER ACTIVITIES

In groups of 5, each coach will present 1 of the following 5 activities (pictures):

In activities #1 and #2 instruct the 2 partners in your group to do 5 push-ups while joined in 2 different ways

1. **One partner holding other partner's ankles**

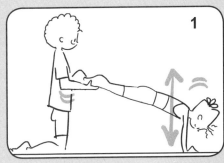

2. **One partner with hands on partner's shoulders**

In activities #3, #4, #5, each pair sits up at the same time and they shake hands

3. **Partners sitting facing each other, toes touching**
   - Alternate shaking left then right hand each sit-up

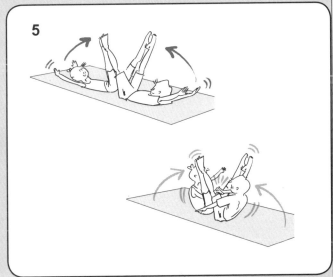

4. **One partner has feet on other partner's knees**
   - Both sit up at same time and clap hands together
   - Each partner takes a turn with feet elevated

5. **Both partners sit-up together and reach between their legs to shake hands**
   - This is quite difficult to do and will require some practice

Counter Balances in pairs

In groups of 7, each coach presents 1 of the 7 activities shown on the next 2 pages.

1. *Back-to-back*

- Partners start standing back to back with arms hooked
- Move your feet away from each other and lean back
- Lean back against each other as you lower slowly to sit
- Lean back against each other as you rise slowly to stand
- Repeat 3 times, stopping ½ up on the last one,
- Hold 10 seconds before standing

2. *Face-to-face*

- Partners start facing each other, hands joined by grasping each other's wrists
- With toes touching, lean backward until arms are straight
- Both partners lean backward and slowly bend knees to sit on floor
- Lean backward and rise slowly to a stand
- Repeat 3 times, stopping ½ way up on the last one
- Hold 10 seconds before standing

3. *Stand on sitting partner*

- Partners start with 1 sitting on box top or bench back against wall
- Other partner faces sitting partner
- Both grasp each other's wrists
- Standing partner steps 1 foot at a time onto sitting partner's knees
- Once standing on sitting partner's knees, straighten arms and lean backward
- If stable, top partner leans more to help sitting partner raise off bench
- Hold 5 seconds before jumping both feet to floor
- Make sure to continue holding wrists as you jump down

Cooperative Locomotions in Pairs

4. Crab walks in pairs

- One partner starts in crab walk position, 2nd partner then takes crab walk position but is connected to 1st partner.

- Feet could be on knees, or on shoulders, or hands could be on knees.

- Or shoulders, or hands, and feet could be on partner (2 high).

5. Monkey walks in pairs

- One partner starts in monkey walk position (front support, body piked).

- 2nd partner then takes monkey walk position but is connected to 1st partner.

- Hands of 2nd partner can be on feet of 1st partner, 2nd partner can be on top of 1st partner, but with hands on floor, etc.

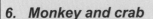

6. Monkey and crab

- One partner in monkey walk.

- Second partner joined but in crab walk.

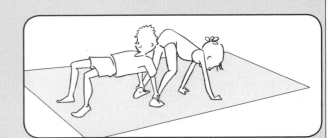

7. Tarantula in pairs

- Partners sit back to back, arms linked.

- They lean back against each other and rise to ½ stand.

- In this ½ stand position they attempt to walk sideways in 1 direction (only their 4 feet are in contact with floor).

List more activities

Ideas on Cooperative Activities generated by the group.

List

PLAY GUIDELINE #4

Tag Games Can Be Your Best Friend

The thousands of different tag games can be divided into 4 groupings.

Remember to always choose safe games in which all participants are always active.

For safety, reduce running speed by having participants locomote by: springing on 2 feet, animal walks, fast walking etc.

Types of tag games

GROUP A	Chasers	Stay the same
GROUP B	Chasers	Accumulate
GROUP C	Caught players	Accumulate
GROUP D	Chased	Immune

Group A   Number of chasers stays the same

These relatively simple tag games are those in which the chaser tags another participant who then becomes the new chaser, and the old chaser then joins the rest of the group being chased.

There can, of course, be several chasers at the same time thus encouraging greater activity. In these simple tag games the number of chasers remains the same throughout the game.

Making it more vigorous

You can make the game more vigorous by changing the manner in which the group LOCOMOTES.

For example, if everyone must spring on 2 feet, the game becomes instantly more physically demanding. Or if everyone is doing monkey running (hands and feet), it is even more strenuous than hopping on 2 feet.

Activity - Crabs and monkeys

Try the following:

Chasers (2-3) are monkeys, and the rest of the group are crabs.

When caught, crabs turn into monkeys and become chasers. The monkey turns into a crab.

C = crab

List

List your activities

In groups of 4, make up other locomotion combinations for this game.

Group B   Number of Chasers Accumulates

In these accumulation tag games, the number of chasers accumulates as the game progresses.

1.   *Catch one, catch all*

- In Catch one, Catch all, 1 person starts as the only chaser and those who are tagged raise one hand, designating them as new chasers.

- The number of chasers quickly accelerates until everyone is a chaser.

2.   *Snakes and frogs*

- One or two players begin as snakes that slither or roll about

- The rest of the group hops about as frogs

- Once tagged, the frogs become snakes and the catcher remains as a snake

- The number of chasers quickly accumulates.

3.   *Chain tag*

- In Chain Tag, 1 to 3 players begin as individual chasers while the rest of the group are chased. When a chaser tags someone, they join hands and pursue others.

- When a 3rd person is caught they also join hands so you now have a chain of three.

- When a 4th person is caught the chain breaks into 2 pairs which each continue to chase others.

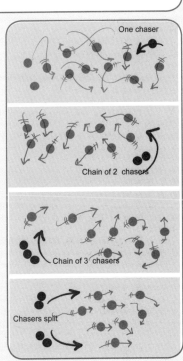

One chaser

Chain of 2 chasers

Chain of 3 chasers

Chasers split

Safety

The chains never get longer than 4 persons, which is much safer than having long chains whipping around.

Variations

And remember, you can vary the mode of locomotion to slow the game and make it safer and to place greater physical demands on participants.

Group C - Number of those Caught Accumulates

Another type of accumulation tag has the persons tagged taking some position that indicates they have been caught.

In our context this would be a STATIONARY POSITION to promote strength, or a flexibility position, or a balance (such as front support, V-balance (tucked), 1 foot balance, splits).

The object of these types of accumulation tag games is to have the chasers catch everyone.

The game can be made more interesting by having some mechanism whereby untagged participants can free those already caught.

For example, if those caught are in front support, they could be freed if someone crawls underneath them. Similarly, if the caught person is holding a V-balance (tucked) they could be freed if someone shakes their hand.

Caught player holds position

Caught players accumulate in number

Eventually all players are caught

Frozen tag

- In Frozen tag – 2 or 3 gymnasts start as the only chasers

- Those who are tagged must stop (freeze) in the positions that were called

- For example, the frozen positions could be: front support, back support, long hang, V balance (tucked), etc.

Never choose headstand or shoulder balance

- The game ends when everyone is caught (frozen)

- You can also have some way that the 'frozen' players can be set free by untagged players to make game more interesting and demanding. For example, a light tap on the shoulder.

Group D - Chased can have immunity from being tagged

A fourth category of tag games that is rich in possibilities for gymnastics classes is immunity tag. In these games, players are immune from being tagged if they are doing some designated activities.

For example:

- push-ups;
- holding a V-sit with straight legs while grasping your ankles;
- holding a bent arm front support,
- hanging from some apparatus.

As you can see, the immunity tasks should be physically and / or technically challenging.

Once the chaser passes by a tagged player, the player can resume running (or whatever locomotion is designated).

The player can choose to stay in the immunity position / activity. If the immunity position is carefully selected, the more time spent in it, the greater the fitness gain for the participant.

PLAY GUIDELINE #5

Games Must be Age and Maturity Appropriate

While it may seem obvious that games should be age appropriate and maturity appropriate, it is often NOT the case. This is especially true if the class comprises participants of various ages.

Activity

In groups of 3, recall examples where games were inappropriate for the group of participants.

Choosing the best games is a matter of common sense and experience. Be alert to inappropriate selection of games.

List
....
....
....
....

PLAY GUIDELINE #6

Quickly Change a Game if Not Working Correctly or if Not Safe

If you find a game is not age or maturity appropriate, then change it quickly. Likewise, if you see any unexpected risks to the participants — change the game quickly. And, of course, if the game is not working as it should (e.g. too many participants being inactive, etc.) then immediately stop the game and make the necessary modifications. You may need more chasers in a tag game, for example.

PLAY GUIDELINE #7

Stop the Game While Children Still Want to Play it

Never play a game too long or too many times in succession as it may begin to get boring. A game stopped while enthusiasm for it is high is a game you can use again. And, participants who are still enthralled with a game will play more vigorously.

Remember, kill a game before it dies!

PLAY GUIDELINE #8

Games should have a purpose.

Coaches should choose games for functional purposes - NOT JUST FOR FUN. Games should enhance physical and motor functions or develop GMP skills.

Instructions - starting the game

At the beginning of any game, always CLEARLY explain the following:

- What mode of Locomotion will be used throughout the game
- What is the function of the chaser(s) when runners are tagged
- How is the chaser(s) identified
- What is function of runners when caught
- Safety precautions

Notes
Refer to the Teaching and Learning Chapter for class management tips.

4

Fitness

FITNESS

Introduction

We stated earlier that the Educational Philosophy of Gymnastics Canada Coach Education is to promote **Fun, Fitness and Fundamentals**. Now we will study the second item in our Educational Philosophy — **FITNESS**.

If participants develop greater fitness in: endurance, strength, power, flexibility, agility, balance, coordination, spatial awareness, etc., they will more successfully learn gymnastics skills (fundamentals).

The more you can design activities to physically challenge participants, the more the body will adapt and the more robust they will become. That will not only promote healthier participants, but will also facilitate successful participation in whatever sports, gymnastics or otherwise, they choose in the future.

The following should provide you with a basic understanding of how the body responds to stimuli to the physical and **motor components** of **FITNESS**.

FITNESS - PHYSICAL COMPONENTS

Your body responds to physical stimuli (or load) by adapting to those stimuli. The tissues naturally prepare themselves for future stresses of a similar level. Your bones, ligaments (which connect bones to bones), muscles, and tendons (which connect muscles to bones) are all highly responsive to physical stimuli (loads).

When stimulated appropriately, muscles can increase their ability to contract repetitively (ENDURANCE) or increase their size and contraction efficiency (STRENGTH & POWER) or increase their length (FLEXIBILITY).

These 4 physical **components of fitness** (endurance, strength, power, and flexibility - ESP&F) are also referred to as the 4 S's (stamina, strength, speed strength, suppleness).

ESP+F	**=**	**4S's**
Endurance		**S**tamina
Strength		**S**trength
Power		**S**peed strength
Flexibility		**S**uppleness

ENDURANCE

Endurance (Muscular)

This component of fitness is the ability of muscle fibres to resist fatigue. It can be improved by increasing the energy (glycogen) stored in the muscle fibres and by increasing the ability to mobilize stored energy from the blood and liver. It is not highly trainable in children.

A good way to stimulate improvement in muscular endurance is to fatigue the muscles with 15 or more repetitive contractions (repetitions).

It is very important for children to develop good **muscular endurance** before, or as, they develop strength. Muscular endurance training prepares the tissues for safer and more efficient strength and power development later.

Many ways of increasing muscular endurance are available through games and fun activities in gymnastics settings.

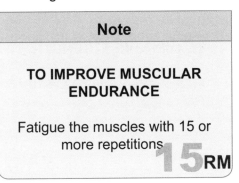

Note
TO IMPROVE MUSCULAR ENDURANCE
Fatigue the muscles with 15 or more repetitions **15**RM

Endurance (Cardiorespiratory)

This component of fitness is the ability of the heart, vessels and lungs to deliver blood (and oxygen) to the muscles. It is well-developed and very trainable in children and as for muscular endurance training, CR endurance training is useful for preparing the tissues for subsequent strength and power training.

You develop this component by doing vigorous activity over several minutes (so the participants are perspiring and breathing deeply). Games with weight bearing, of a continuous nature, are excellent.

Complete Q6 & Q7

STRENGTH

This component of fitness is the maximum force a muscle generates in a single contraction. It can be increased if we increase the size of the muscle (more contractile protein inside the fibre) or if we increase the neural efficiency of the muscle. Strength is very trainable in children, especially as the result of neural improvement.

When describing strength training techniques, we will often use the term Repetitions Maximum (RM). This is the number of repetitions that can be performed until exhaustion.

For example, if you can only perform an exercise 1 time, then that weight (or load) is called your 1RM. If it takes 10 repetitions before the muscle is exhausted, then that load is deemed to be your 10RM load.

Children in community sport and educational gymnastics settings should increase their strength by doing activities in the 10 to 15 RM range. That is, their climbing, traversing, swinging, jumping, pushing up, chinning up, sitting up etc., can often be done in a game context and will develop strength if the children fatigue after 10 -15 repetitions.

Muscle contraction and muscle length

The following 3 'bullets' describe 3 different mechanical states of muscle contraction. Understanding these will take on greater importance in subsequent levels of coach education.

- When a muscle contracts and there is NO change in its length (no movement), it is called the **isometric state**.
- If a muscle contracts and shortens (as when lifting a weight or moving body upwards) it is called the **concentric state** (note 'o' in 'shorten' and in 'concentric').
- If a muscle contracts and lengthens (as in lowering a weight or lowering the body) this is called the **eccentric state** (note 'e' in 'eccentric' and in 'lengthen').

Note

TO IMPROVE STRENGTH

With children choose the 10-15 RM range. **10-15**RM

Complete Q8

POWER

This component of fitness is the combination of strength and speed. It is a measure of how fast we can generate maximum force. We can enhance power by doing activities very quickly.

Contracting muscles both very hard and very fast can result in injuries. It is, therefore, prudent to spend several years preparing the body's tissues by building endurance, strength and speed before specifically training Power. Only after the tissues are well conditioned should we train both high resistance and high speed.

FLEXIBILITY

If muscles and tendons are stretched, painlessly but frequently, those tissues will adapt by increasing their resting length. This in turn increases the Range of Motion (R.O.M) about the joint(s) the muscles cross. We call this FLEXIBILITY and it is highly trainable in children.

Passive R.O.M

This R.O.M is achieved using external forces.

Active R.O.M

This R.O.M uses the internal force of muscle contraction. Obtaining a good ACTIVE RANGE (needed for most gymnastics skills) requires that you utilize equal amounts of strength training and stretching training.

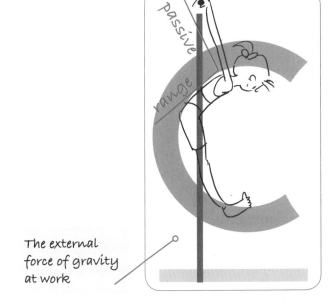

The external force of gravity at work

NOTE

Over-stretching does NOT achieve good ACTIVE RANGES.

Physical components and the course

We will continually refer to these above physical qualities throughout the rest of the course and we will have many opportunities to practise activities that enhance these physical qualities.

MUSCLE FUNCTION

Since muscle contraction is the basis of all movement, and thus the basis of all gymnastics skills and physical preparation, it is helpful for us to understand this tissue and its functions.

A muscle fibre is a long thin cell about the diameter of a human hair that has the unique ability to shorten (contract) when a neural signal stimulates it. The shortening is due to contractile filaments (proteins) sliding over each other.

There are basically 2 types of muscle fibres, those that contract very fast but run out of energy quickly (fast twitch fibres) and those that contract more slowly but do not fatigue as quickly (slow twitch fibres).

Most people have equal distribution of these 2 types of fibres but some people have greater proportions of one or the other.

What would be the effect of having a much greater ratio of fast twitch fibres than average?

Q | Complete   Q9

FITNESS - MOTOR COMPONENTS

Besides the above 4 "physical" components of FITNESS (ESP & F), there are also many complex neural (or motor) phenomenon such as: AGILITY, BALANCE, COORDINATION (many kinds) and SPATIAL ORIENTATION (ABC'S). These 'motor' components of fitness are also trainable - given the appropriate stimuli.

ABC's

- Agility
- Balance
- Coordination
- Spatial orientation

FITNESS - MOTOR COMPONENTS

AGILITY

This is a complex capacity to move the body quickly and efficiently from position to position and from place to place. It is enhanced by repetitive activities involving whole body movements as seen in games, and in tumbling and vaulting.

BALANCE

This is a complex ability to hold stationary positions and to move while in a balanced state (dynamic balance). It relies on sensory functions of the Kinesthetic Sense, the Tactile Sense, as well as muscular strength (rigidity) and flexibility. The Kinesthetic Sense comprises 2 separate sensory systems of the body:

- The Proprioceptive System, which signals where your limbs are relative to your body
- The Vestibular System, which signals where your body is in space

COORDINATION

There are many kinds of Coordination:

- Whole body coordination involves the whole body moving in complex patterns such as cartwheels, saltos, dance steps, complex jumps or leaps. Many skills in gymnastics are examples of complex Coordination activities.
- Hand-eye, and foot-eye coordination involves manipulating projectiles or implements such as balls, clubs, etc.

All gymnastics sports demand high levels of Coordination and, in turn, they all develop high levels of Coordination.

SPATIAL ORIENTATION

This motor component is related to balance and sensitivity to the body being inverted and spinning free in space. It is associated with the Vestibular part of the Kinesthetic Sense. It is enhanced by many of the activities that we typically do in gymnastics sports.

SUMMARY

Training and improving these **physical** and **motor** components of FITNESS is the very essence of improving skills in all gymnastics sports. The more we understand how our body's tissues respond to positive stimuli, the more effective we will be in coaching.

We stated that the Educational Philosophy of Gymnastics Canada's Coach Education is to promote **Fun, Fitness**, and **Fundamentals**.

We have just been studying the FITNESS component and we will now move to the last component - **FUNDAMENTALS**.

Since we are going to be analyzing commonalities in movement patterns of all the different gymnastics sports it will serve us well to take a short detour into the history of each of the sports.

5

Origins of Gymnastics

WHAT IS GYMNASTICS?

You will see on the next few pages that all modern gymnastics sports share some common historical origins. This first course is primarily about examining the distinguishing features or 'commonalities' and helping you appreciate the similarities in all Gymnastics Sports. Subsequent courses in each sport will examine how they have diverged from one another and how each is unique.

Do you know?

- How many Gymnastics sports exist?
- What makes Gymnastics sports different from other sports?
- The origins of the different Gymnastics sports?
- The 'events' of each Gymnastics sport?
- When the first 'competition' was held?
- Where (country) each 'event' originated?
- Who are the fathers (and mothers) of Gymnastics?
- Who are some of our champions (past and current)?

Early records

There are records and art works depicting gymnastics type activities being done in ancient China, Egypt, Greece, and Rome. As it turns out, most modern Gymnastics sports evolved from 4 main sources:

1. Military
2. Education
3. Medical
4. Performing Arts

HISTORICAL ORIGIN #1 - MILITARY

Several gymnastics events have very clear origins in military training. Let's look at four:

Rings in Men's Artistic Gymnastics

This event was formerly called Roman Rings. But why Roman Rings? Well, as you might have guessed, the Romans used rings as a conditioning apparatus for soldiers and gladiators.

Pommel Horse in Men's Artistic Gymnastics

This event also had its origins in the training of soldiers. The pommel horse evolved from wooden and leather replicas of real horses that were used, in many cultures, to safely train soldiers how to mount, dismount and use weapons (swords, lances, etc.) on horseback. The 'pommels', of course, were the front and back parts of the saddle.

Vault in Artistic Gymnastics

The earliest vaulting devices were wooden horses used to train soldiers in the mounting and remounting of horses. Wooden horses were also used in schools and training academies to teach ladies how to mount, ride and dismount correctly.

Clubs in Rhythmic Gymnastics

This might be a surprise, but the original clubs that were swung in gymnasia 200-300 years ago were called Indian Clubs. They were of various sizes and weights and were used to physically condition soldiers for sabre swinging. Rows of various sized Indian Clubs were common in many physical education equipment rooms up until 30 or 40 years ago and are still seen in older gyms around the world.

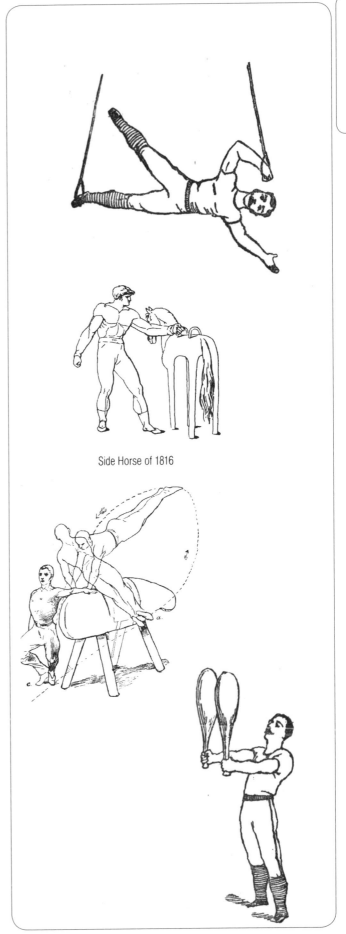

Side Horse of 1816

HISTORICAL ORIGIN #2 – EDUCATION

Several modern gymnastics events and apparatus were invented or popularized by European educators responsible for ensuring that their students were physically, as well as mentally, robust.

The German educator Johann Freidrich GutsMuths and his student Friedrich Ludwig Jahn are considered the 'grandfathers' of Artistic Gymnastics putting into place formal systems of physical preparation and inventing apparatus such as Horizontal Bar and Parallel Bars.

Their influence spread to Scandinavia where Pehr Henrik Ling developed sophisticated routines that systematically trained the body. The Swedish form of gymnastics was actually a very systematic development of the body's musculature through the use of rhythmical sequences of calisthenics. It was also strongly influenced by the fluid movements in Fencing.

The exercises were roughly divided into 'free exercises' and 'apparatus exercises'. The 'free' or 'floor' exercise in Artistic Gymnastics and the 'calisthenics' of Aerobic Gymnastics and some hand apparatus in Rhythmic Gymnastics have a direct lineage back to these times.

As these Swedish and German systems were transplanted to other countries, local adaptations took place. Many of these 'fitness' apparatus were eventually formalized into general educational practice and became modern day Parallel Bars, Horizontal Bar, Balance Beam and even Pole Vault.

When the various schools and teachers' training academies exhibited their students' performances in festivals and competitions, modern gymnastics sports began to evolve and spread throughout Europe and the world.

WOMAN'S GYMNASTIC COSTUME IN 1842
Copied from an old picture.

HISTORICAL ORIGIN #3 – MEDICAL

Many educators were also medical practitioners and the exercises and systems of training that they developed were also used in the prevention and the rehabilitation of injuries, particularly after the 1st and 2nd World Wars.

The very early physical therapy practitioners were gymnastics educators and they developed exercise therapy protocols, such as Pilates.

HISTORICAL ORIGIN #4 – PERFORMING ARTS

The 4th and probably oldest source of modern gymnastics is from the Performing Arts. Many cultures developed performing artists that included tumblers, vaulters and other aerial acrobats. Chinese, Egyptian and Greek (Minoan) pottery from more than 2000 years ago, depict highly skilled acrobats.

Many of the performing groups incorporated tumbling, hand balancing (Acrobatic Gymnastics), and the use of springing devices, teeter boards and swings. Some of these apparatus were subsequently adopted by educators and appeared in the earliest gymnasia.

The tradition of gymnastics activities being part of the entertainment repertoire continues today in many activities such as cheerleading, circus groups (Cirque du Soleil), stage productions and movies.

FIG. 3.—EGYPTIAN BALL GAME.

know this ....

ORIGINS OF EACH GYMNASTICS SPORT

Acrobatic Gymnastics (AcG)

This gymnastics sport is basically hand balancing or adagio as it is known in the circus world. This ancient gymnastics art form has 5 events in its modern competitive version:

- Men's Pairs
- Women's Pairs
- Mixed Pairs
- Women's 3's
- Men's 4's

Aerobic Gymnastics (AG)

The origins of Aerobic Gymnastics are the same as Artistic and Rhythmic Gymnastics. The systematic Swedish gymnastics and its free flowing calisthenics spawned many modern variants.

While the contemporary fitness industry in North America has been mainly fixated on the weight lifting and exercise machine usage, the European tradition of calisthenics is a clear precursor to the modern sport of Aerobic Gymnastics.

The Aerobics Gymnastics events, as governed and regulated by the International Gymnastics Federation (F.I.G.), contain the following categories:

- Individual Male and Individual Female
- Mixed Pairs
- Trios
- Groups of 6 Gymnasts

Artistic Gymnastics

As we have seen, the sport now called Artistic Gymnastics evolved from military (pommel horse, rings, vault), performing arts (tumbling, balancing), and educational and medical origins (beam, horizontal bar, parallel bars, floor exercise). It became a more focused sport with the reintroduction of the Olympic Games in 1896.

Men's Artistic Gymnastics (MAG)

Men's Artistic Gymnastics was included in the 1st Modern Olympics (1896). Eventually 6 events were chosen to highlight the 'all-around' man for the Olympics.

The apparatus were chosen to demonstrate development of the legs (tumbling and vault), development of the upper body in support (pommel horse and parallel bars), and development of the upper body in suspension (rings and horizontal bar).

From the 1924 Olympics, the Olympic competitive order was established as:

- Floor Exercise
- Pommel Horse
- Rings
- Vault
- Parallel Bars
- Horizontal Bar

Women's Artistic Gymnastics (WAG)

While the female events were not added until the 1928 Olympics, it must be remembered that females were participating in gymnastics much earlier. Depending on the country and school, they may have participated in 'free' exercise and/or apparatus training. These exercises often incorporated dance. Additionally, the use of balance beam for developing poise, elegance and 'good carriage' is well documented.

The 4 events that were adopted for Olympic competition for Women's Artistic Gymnastics were:

- Vault
- Asymmetric Bars
- Balance Beam
- Floor Exercise

FIG. 216. — INSIDE POMMEL-VAULT WITH FREE SUPPORTS.

Women's Gymnastics in 1845 at Bale, Switzerland

Rhythmic Gymnastics (RG)

Rhythmic Gymnastics has very similar origins to Women's Artistic Gymnastics. Women's Colleges incorporated many gymnastics activities including Swedish calisthenics, and the use of hand apparatus to promote fitness, rhythm, grace, and poise. Dance was very often equally as important in the physical education curriculum as was gymnastics and the 2 were often combined which, of course, is the origin of modern Rhythmic Gymnastics.

The contemporary sport has 5 hand apparatus, a 'free event' and a group event. The 5 hand apparatus, in Olympic order, are:

- Rope
- Hoop
- Balls
- Clubs
- Ribbon

Rhythmic Gymnastics was first included in the 1984 Olympic Games where Lori Fung of Canada was the Olympic Gold medalist.

While there is a long tradition of men also doing group calisthenics and using hand apparatus, this is rarely seen outside of the gymnastics festivals. An exception is the Japanese Men's University teams, which still compete in group Rhythmic events.

Trampoline Gymnastics (TG)

Trampoline is the newest apparatus in the gymnastics family. The modern trampoline was invented in the 1930's but it has ancient roots in performers striving to gain additional airtime by using some springing or throwing device. Many devices have been developed:

- Blanket or Hide Throw (Inuit, etc.)
- Teeter Board
- Spring Board (including diving boards)
- Russian Swings
- Trapeze

While there are several precursors, the direct antecedent of the modern trampoline was assembled in 1936 by circus acrobats and divers George Nissen and Larry Griswold.

The sport was a popular American intercollegiate sport and spread throughout the world. The first World Championships in Trampoline was held in 1964. The first time Trampoline was included in the Olympics was at the 2000 Sydney Games with an Individual Women's and Men's Trampoline competition. At that time, Canada won 2 bronze medals (Karen Cockburn and Mathieu Turgeon).

Other events in TG include:

- Synchronized Men's and Women's Trampoline
- Double Mini-Trampoline for Men and Women
- Tumbling for Men and Women

THE ENGLISH BOARD.

Gymnastics for All (GfA)

Gymnastics for All has a rich heritage of large groups performing Gymnastics in exhibitions and festivals. In many Socialist countries, large national celebrations include mass displays of gymnastics. The great gymnastics festivals of Europe are predominantly group gymnastics. Some of these big festivals are:

- World Gymnaestrada held every 4 years with over 20,000 performing participants
- German, Swiss and Austrian Turnfests
- Czech and Slovak Sokol Slets
- Scandinavian Landsstvne

SUMMARY

The Many Faces of Gymnastics

All Gymnastics sports have evolved from similar historical roots and all continue to change and branch. There are also several other sports and activities that fall under the umbrella of Gymnastics (Team Gymnastics, Martial Gymnastics, and Aesthetic Gymnastics). Also Cheerleading is a member organization in some Federations.

In addition, there are elaborate systems of 'educational gymnastics' in many countries that often form the core of physical education programs.

There are also thousands of recreational gymnastics programs that are not codified as the sports are, but that are the building blocks and financial lifeblood of many of the Gymnastics sports. These include many types of exhibition or display gymnastics, pre-school gymnastics, recreational gymnastics, applied (to other sports) gymnastics and fall under the broad heading of Gymnastics for All.

THE CONTENT OF THIS COURSE

This first Foundations course in Gymnastics will give all participants - those from the major sports and those seeking basic training in educational and recreational gymnastics - a greater understanding of each other. The course will also provide greater sharing of ideas and knowledge than the previous separate gymnastics coaching courses offered.

We will now study the final component in our Educational Philosophy – FUNDAMENTALS. It may seem strange to put FUNDAMENTALS as the last of our philosophical goals, but ensuring participants are having FUN and increasing their FITNESS are essential precursors to teaching them good fundamentals. After all, if participants do not enjoy gymnastics (FUN), they will not stay in gymnastics, and if they are not physically prepared (FITNESS), they will be less successful and less likely to continue in Gymnastics.

Fundamentals

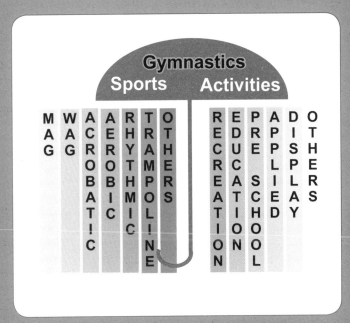

FUNDAMENTAL MOVEMENT PATTERNS

Our task now is to see if we can find some commonality in the tens of thousands of skills from the many sports and activities called GYMNASTICS.

What are the FUNDAMENTALS that all gymnastics sports share?

Imagine a great hall with several hundred gymnasts from all gymnastics sports and activities performing at the same time.

Are there some common patterns of movement that all the skills and activities share?

Yes. For a start, we can mechanically divide all the gymnastics skills into 2 groups – skills that are stationary, and skills that are not stationary.

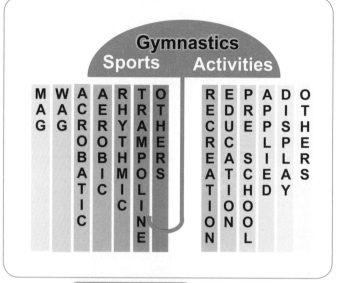

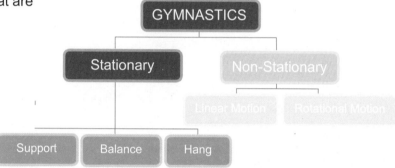

Group 1 – GYMNAST IS STATIONARY

Mechanically, STATIONARY skills are performed within the gymnast's base of support. That is, the gymnast's centre of mass does not move outside the base of support.

If the centre of mass is centered over the base of support, the gymnast will be stable and we will call these skills supports.

If the centre of mass is near the edge of the base of support, the gymnast will be unstable, and we will call these skills balances.

If the centre of mass is below the base of support, the gymnast will be very stable, and we will call these skills hangs.

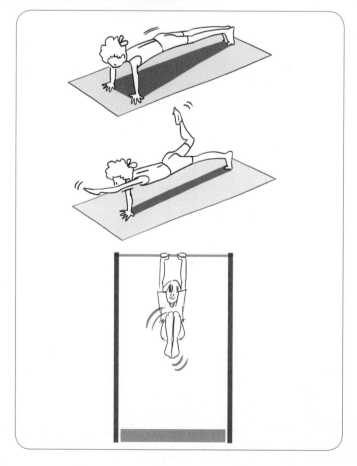

Statics or stationary?

In previous courses, the FMP STATIONARY was called STATICS. This has been changed because 'static' means no-movement and 'dynamic' means movement. You can be STATIONARY (centre of mass inside base) and be either static or dynamic. For example, you can be holding a balance position while dynamically doing body waves or manipulating hand apparatus. You are clearly not 'static', but you are STATIONARY.

Similarly, when you press up to a headstand, you are clearly not static, but you are stationary because your centre of mass stays inside your base. You are stationary, but not static.

Group 2 – GYMNAST is NON-STATIONARY

Mechanically this means skills are performed while the *base of support is moving* or, the skill is performed *'outside'* the gymnast's base of support.

This group can be divided further into 2 movement subgroups of skills that are:

a)   LINEAR in nature

b)   ROTATIONAL in nature

a) LINEAR

Skills, in which the path of the centre of mass is of a LINEAR nature, can be mechanically sub-divided into 2 movement patterns:

Non-Stationary
- Linear Motion
  - Spring
  - Locomotion
- Rotational Motion

1. **Spring** - skills that are moving from their base of support in a single explosive movement. Other terms are take-off, leap, jump, hop, etc.

2. **Locomotion** – skills moving from base of support in repetitive movements. Other terms are running, skipping, dance steps, traversing, climbing, etc.

Non-Stationary
- Linear motion
- Rotational Motion
  - Rotation
  - Swing

b) ROTATIONAL

Skills where the path of the gymnast's centre of mass is of a ROTATIONAL nature can be mechanically sub-divided into 2 movement patterns:

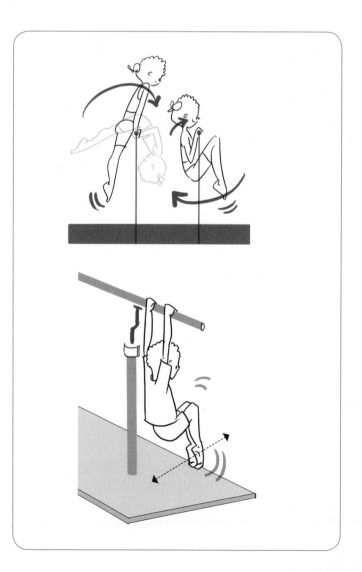

1. **Rotation** – skills that are rotating about one of the body's 3 internal axes. Other terms are: saltos, twists, spins, pivots, turns, rolls, pirouettes, etc.

> **Question**
>
> Can you see that ROTATION can occur while free-in-space *or* while in contact with base of support?

2. **Swing** – skills that are rotating about an external axis (such as bars and rings).

Group 3 – FROM MOTION TO STATIONARY

LANDINGS are skills in which the centre of mass is moving 'to' the base of support. It is mechanically the opposite of SPRING since it involves the absorption of energy.

This is one of the most common movement patterns in all gymnastics sports, and the most important of all from a safety perspective.

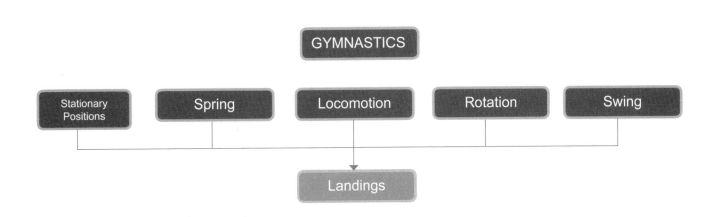

Common mechanical principles

In each of the 6 Fundamental Movement Patterns, the mechanical principles are common *for all skills within that movement pattern.*

Understanding a few mechanical principles about these few movement patterns, allows us to understand tens of thousands of skills from all the sports and activities of Gymnastics.

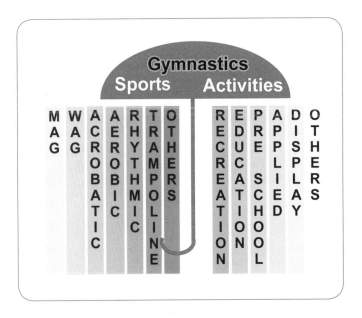

Group 4 – GYMNAST & HAND APPARATUS

Rhythmic gymnasts will be: STATIONARY, or SPRINGING, or LOCOMOTING, or ROTATING or SWINGING, or, LANDING, *but they will also be manipulating hand apparatus.*

The mechanics of the motion of the hand apparatus are the same as that of the gymnasts' motion. The hand apparatus will be:

- STATIONARY - balancing
- SPRINGING - throwing, bouncing, pushing
- LOCOMOTING - dribbling, rolling
- ROTATING - spinning, wrapping
- SWINGING – limbs swinging apparatus
- LANDING – catching, trapping

Q | Complete   *Q10*

7

Stationary Positions

STATIONARY POSITIONS

ℚ | Complete ℚ11 & ℚ12

Mechanics of STATIONARY POSITIONS

All the STATIONARY (Static) skills in gymnastics sports have one thing in common: the body's Centre of Mass remains within the body's Base of Support. The term "base of support" is self explanatory but *centre of mass* is a concept that needs some explanation.

Let's look at the *centre of mass* of an object (a clipboard) to help understand this concept.

Centre of Mass (Centre of Gravity)

Place a clipboard so the long side balances on the edge of your outstretched forefinger (held as if you are pointing at something).

Draw a line on the clipboard where it was balanced on your finger. Now turn the clipboard so that the short side balances on your outstretched forefinger, and again draw a line.

Where these 2 lines intersect you should be able to balance the clipboard on your fingertip.

Definitions of Centre of Mass

Definition 1
The balance point of a body = its Centre of Mass.

Definition 2
Another definition of Centre of Mass = 'the point about which all the body's mass is equally distributed in all directions'.

Balance point

Definition 3

A 3rd way of describing Centre of Mass is very useful for gymnastics coaches because it is: 'the point about which a body rotates when it is free in space'.

Activity ...

Put several small round chalk marks (or coloured pen) on the surface of the clipboard, including one at the Centre of Mass.

Throw the clipboard so it is spinning end over end into the air. The Centre of Mass point will remain in the centre of the spinning clipboard while the rest of the clipboard and the other points will spin around it.

That is, the centre of mass is the point about which the clipboard is rotating.

Definition 4

The final definition of Centre of Mass is also useful for gymnastics coaches because it is 'the intersection of the 3 primary axes'.

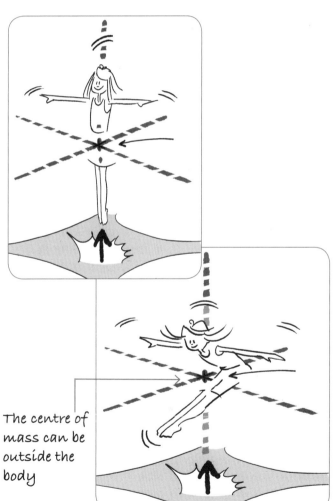

The centre of mass can be outside the body

Note

The Centre of Mass of a body is not a fixed point. It varies as the body mass distribution varies. If you are standing and you raise your arms in the air, your mass is shifted upward, so therefore the Centre of Mass is also shifted upward.

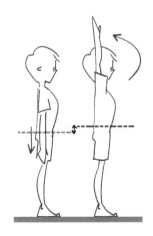

Categories of STATIONARY positions

In answering Questions 11 and 12, you probably grouped some STATIONARY POSITONS as 'balances' (handstands, levers, arabesques etc.) and some skills as 'supports' (front support as in push up, seat support as in seat drop, bridge support, etc.) and some skills as 'hangs' (long hang, glide hang, etc.)

STATIONARY POSITIONS - 3 CATEGORIES

Support

Hang

Balance

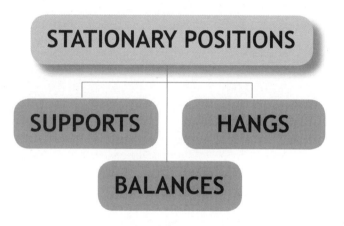

STATIONARY POSITIONS

SUPPORTS   **HANGS**

BALANCES

1. Supports

Mechanically, if your Centre of Mass is near the middle of your base of support, you are very stable and we will call such skills SUPPORTS.

To demonstrate this, hold a front support, (stable) then lift your right arm and left leg off the ground. You will now be in a BALANCE (unstable).

In the BALANCE opposite, the Centre of Mass is closer to the edge of the base of support and is more unstable than the front support.

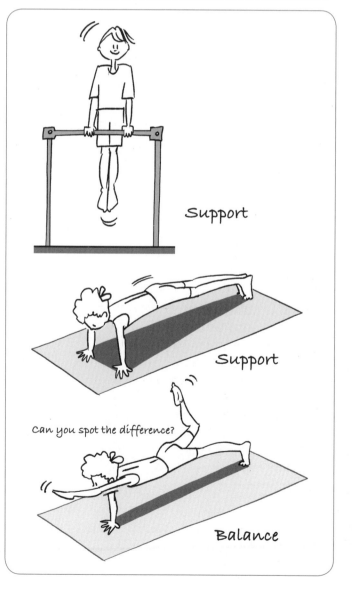

Support

Support

Can you spot the difference?

Balance

2. Balances

If your Centre of Mass is near the edge of your base of support, a small amount of movement can cause it to move outside your base of support and you will no longer be STATIONARY. When your Centre of Mass is close to the edge of your base, you are unstable and we will call all such skills BALANCES.

3. Hangs

The final mechanical grouping of STATIONARY POSITIONS are those skills in which the Centre of Mass is directly below the base. These are called Hangs and they are mechanically the most stable of all STATIONARY POSITIONS.

Complete Q13

Aesthetics of STATIONARY Positions

Note

All gymnastics sports are subjectively judged and all have an artistic component that is referred to as: "good form", "artistic interpretation", "artistic merit", etc. The basic aesthetic foundations of 'good form' have evolved in gymnastics sports in a similar manner as in the performing arts (dance and theatre) in that they all have Ballet as the foundational dance form from which most aesthetic traditions evolve.

Mechanics of Good Form

In addition to the historic 'performing arts' interpretation of good form, there is also a group of mechanical reasons for 'good form'. That is, the tighter the body and the closer the body mass is to the rotational axis, the faster the body will spin, or salto, or cartwheel.

Likewise, the more rigid the body, the easier it will balance and the better it will SPRING.
In these cases, 'good form' has biomechanical benefits which may or may not coincide with aesthetic values.

Tight body for control

Mechanics vs aesthetics

There will be examples, of course, where good mechanical technique will not be very aesthetically pleasing. An example is 'cowboying' when tucking knees wide in saltos. The straddled knees allows the mass to be brought closer to the salto axis, but the appearance is not very pleasing (mechanically efficient, aesthetically 'yucky').

Similarly, an arched handstand will lower the centre of mass and make the handstand more stable (as seen in top person in some Acrobatic balances), but again, the aesthetics are debatable and the stress on the back is questionable.

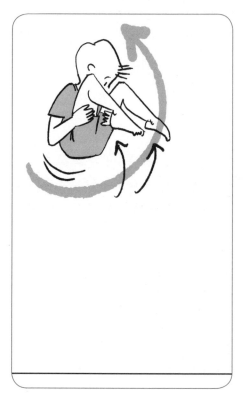

BASIC POSTURAL POSITIONS

Simple postures form the basis of aesthetic movement and in this section you will experience basic postures and develop your "eye" for what is judged to be "good form" in basic postures (STATIONARY positions).

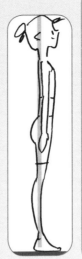

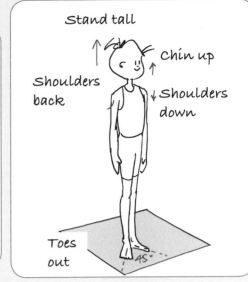

Stand tall

Chin up

Shoulders back

Shoulders down

Toes out

Standing (legs together)

Stand tall and straight,

- With chin slightly up
- All body parts in vertical line
- Shoulders slightly back and lowered in natural position.
- Legs turned out so toes are 45° apart, heels together

Move ARMS to different positions without elevating shoulders

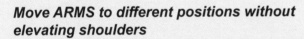

- Move both arms to horizontal sideways
- Arms rounded with hands slightly in front of shoulders (Ballet, WAG and RG)
- Arms straight with hands slightly behind shoulders (MAG T&G)

Move both arms overhead, without elevating shoulders

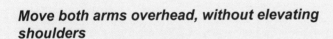

Rounded-Arm Technique (1)
- Slightly bent arms, hands slightly relaxed
- Head up, looking at hands
- Hands slightly in front of shoulders

Straight-Arm Technique (2)
- Straight arms, hands turned out and fingers together and pointed
- Head up looking at hands
- Hands slightly behind shoulders

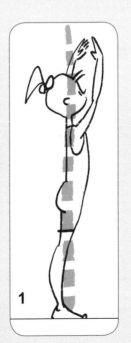

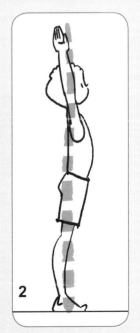

1

2

GYMNASTICS CANADA GYMNASTIQUE

Changing Postures (legs apart)

Straddle stand

Move both legs sidewards (straddle)

- Maintain turn-out from the hips
- Slowly straddle as wide as possible

Stride stand

Move 1 leg forward and 1 leg backward (stride) to lunge

- Bend forward leg 90°
- Make certain both legs turn-out
- Straighten legs to stride stand and lower as far as possible
- Knees over toes

Stride Stand & Turn

From narrow stride stand with arms sideways

- Raise up on toes
- As arms raise overhead
- Follow them with head and eyes
- Do ½ turn on toes
- Finish in stride stand facing opposite direction
- Arms lower sideways as heels lower

Repeat several times,
- Keeping shoulders down,
- Follow hands with head,
- Legs finish in turn-out

Leg Posture While Sitting

Legs together

Straighten your legs so that the backs of your knees touch the floor

- Point the foot, then point the toes
- Some will straighten legs so well that heels come off the floor as back of knees touches
- Press heels, ankles and toes together

Legs straddled

While sitting, straddle your legs wide, and turn-out, bend forward with straight back, arms sideways

- Sit up straight
- Move arms overhead, with head following
- Keep shoulders down
- Vary arm positions

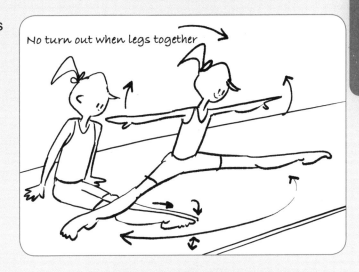

No turn out when legs together

Other Basic Postural Positions & Shapes

Tuck positions

- Sitting, toes pointed, holding tight tuck
- Lying on back, arms overhead, body flat and stretched
- Snap to a tight tuck sit
- Repeat, finishing in squat position, feet flat on floor
- Fairly difficult to do well…

Pike positions - sequence 1

- Sitting, legs on floor, body piked forward
- Sitting, arms behind on floor, pike (V balance)
- Sitting arms sideways, pike (V balance)
- Sitting, hands on floor in front, lift legs to front straddle pike

Sequence 1

Pike positions - sequence 2

- Lying on back, open pike (as back drop position on trampoline)
- Lying on back, tight pike
- Lying on back, tight pike, legs straddled.

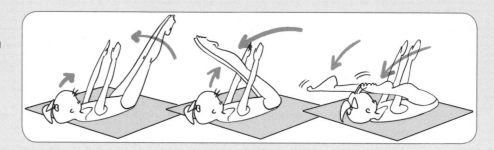

Layout Positions - Banana Shapes

Banana shape (incurve)

Lying on back, arms stretched overhead,

- Stretch long, keep body flat
- Move arms quickly to sides
- Chin on chest, legs & shoulder off ground, banana shape

Banana shape (out curve)

- Shoulder & heels on ground, back arched off floor, banana shape.

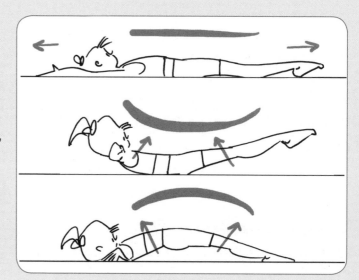

Kneeling Positions

Perform individually or as a sequence

BASIC SUPPORTS

Recall the difference between BALANCES and SUPPORTS

With a partner, alternate watching and doing the following STATIONARY positions:

FRONT SUPPORTS

- Body straight, head in line with body.
- Push down gently on partner's hips to ensure body is rigid.
- Push partner gently side to side to ensure body is rigid.

Front support facing each other

- Partner 1 varies arm positions 5x, partner 2 copies (hold each for 5 seconds)
- Partner 2 varies leg positions 5x, partner 1 copies (hold each for 5 seconds).

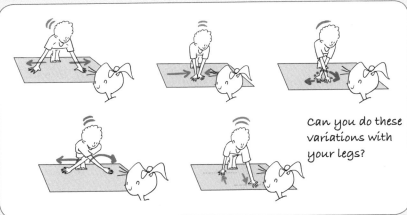

Can you do these variations with your legs?

Front support feet on the wall

One partner leads, while the other partner follows in variations of wall supported front supports.

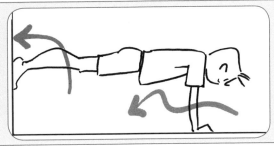

Harder variations

Front support with a partner

Both partners in front support, while in contact with each other.

- 2 points of contact with partner (e.g. 2 hands on partners ankles)
- Do 3 variations of this theme.

More front supports with a partner

Both partners in front support, but only 2 hands and 2 feet (total) in contact with floor. Do 3 variations of this theme.

Show and Tell

Each pair practise, then show your most physically demanding 'structure' to the class.

The whole class tries this 'structure'. This repeats until the whole class tries every pair's 'structure'.

Younger Children

Suggest appropriate modifications to front and back supports suitable for younger children. Write your response here:

_____

_____

_____

_____

BACK SUPPORTS

It would be possible to repeat everything that has been covered in front supports but using back supports.

This may not be done during this course but you should include back support activities in your practical work in your gym.

In pairs try a few combinations of back supports joined to partner. Conclude with the demanding structure shown opposite.

Combine Front & Back Supports

Each pair invents 3 front and back support structures. Some advanced structures are illustrated opposite.

Each pair shows their best structure to the class.

Advanced

Safety

Bridge supports are very valuable for both Fitness and Fundamentals. There are, however, several precautions that must be taken when coaching bridge supports.

Firstly, there is danger of injury if unprepared gymnasts fall or drop into bridges (if they fall backwards from a stand or fall from a handstand into a bridge support). These ways of getting into bridge supports should only be performed after adequate physical preparation and skill progressions have been undertaken.

Bridges are also somewhat age sensitive in that they should NOT be taught to the very young or to older adults.

BRIDGE SUPPORTS

Safe ways to teach bridges

 Bridges should first be introduced from positions where the feet are elevated higher than the hands since there is considerably less arch in the back thus less stress on the back.

Try this ...

With a partner, go around the gym and explore 5 ways of doing bridge supports with feet elevated higher than the hands.

Vary Hand Positions in Bridge Support

Feet up = 'safe back'

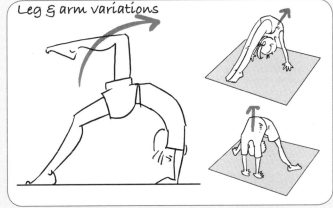

Leg & arm variations

BASIC SUPPORTS

CROSS SUPPORTS in 3s

In groups of 4, each coaches the other 3 on one of the following:

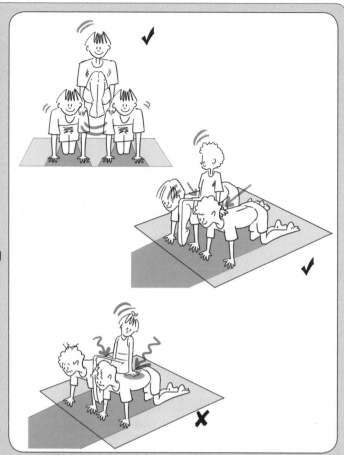

1. The 2 bases are on their hands and knees

- Take turns holding CROSS SUPPORTS on partners' shoulders.

- Take turns holding CROSS SUPPORTS on partners' hips.

- Perform 3 variations in each support (vary leg positions, arm bend, trunk positions).

2. The 2 bases are both kneeling side-by-side

- Take turns holding CROSS SUPPORTS on partners' shoulders.

- Perform 3 variations in each support (vary: leg positions, arm bend, trunk positions).

3. The 2 bases are both lying side-by-side facing up

- Take turns holding CROSS SUPPORTS on top of partners' bent knees.

- Perform 3 variations in each support (vary: leg positions, arm bend, trunk positions).

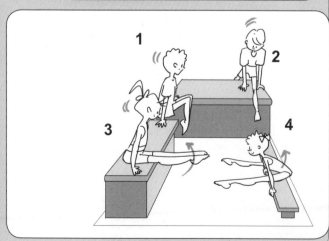

CROSS SUPPORTS ON APPARATUS

4. CROSS SUPPORTS at stations

Each group of 4 goes to a CROSS SUPPORT station (between stacked mats, benches, box horses, etc.) and work on sequence of L CROSS SUPPORTS:

- Tucked L CROSS SUPPORT

- Stride CROSS SUPPORT

- Straight leg L CROSS SUPPORT

- Straddled leg CROSS SUPPORT

BASIC BALANCES

NOTE

Note that basic STATIONARY POSITIONS are the foundation of all gymnastics skills and that they can be excellent for developing the physical qualities and motor qualities (balance, spatial awareness, etc.)

Basic Balances

In groups of 4, one coaches the other 3 on variations of the following (#1- #4 shown here):

SAFETY

Shoulder balances are good for developing both physical qualities (strength, flexibility) and motor qualities (balance, spatial orientation).

For safe teaching:

* Only a few repetitions should be performed each session

* They should NOT be taught to the very young or the older adult.

1. Balances on the Feet 5 variations

2. Balances on the Knees 5 variations

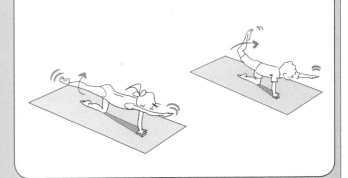

3. Balances on the Seat 5 variations

LEGS	ARMS
• legs bent	• above head
• apart	• behind back
• at different heights	• holding legs or feet

4. Balances on the Shoulders

Leg & arm variations

1 shoulder

BALANCES ON THE HEAD AND HANDS

Safe Teaching

Headstands are good for developing both physical qualities (strength) and motor qualities (balance, spatial orientation), but as with Bridge Supports, you must be cautious when introducing Head-stands.

Only a few repetitions should be performed each session to prevent gymnasts from developing sore necks and, like Bridge Supports, headstands are AGE SENSITIVE and should NOT be taught to the very young or the older adult.

Note

Headstands should NOT be performed on the forehead. The gymnast should balance on the very top of the head such that the cervical (neck) vertebrae are in a straight line. Please note that if the balance is done on the forehead, the cervical vertebrae will be in arched position and this is not as strong or safe as when neck is in a straight line.

The illustration to the right is simply to help you understand placement of the head on the floor. Do NOT do this with your gymnast.

The top of the head, not the forehead, placed on the mat ensures pressure on the neck is minimised

---

SAFETY

✔ Just a few repetitions each session

✔ Do not teach to the very young or old

✔ Balance is on the top of the head NOT the fore-head

HEADSTANDS

In groups of 6, each coaches the other 5 in one of the following (#1- #6 below):

1. *Tripod Balance*

- From kneeling with head and hands on floor (form a triangle)
- Step 1 knee onto 1 elbow
- Then step the other knee onto the other elbow
- Balance on the very top of your head
- Step down from this 'tripod' balance after 3 seconds

2. *Rolling out of Tripod Balance*

- Begin as above by stepping into a tripod balance
- Step down 1 foot and push off that foot and tuck chin to chest
- Roll forward out of the tripod balance
- Next time, push with both arms, tuck chin to chest and roll out of tripod balance

Step one leg down & roll ....

3. *Bipod Balance*

- From squat with knees apart and arms between knees
- Bend elbows outward and squeeze knees into elbows
- Tilt forward and slowly lift your feet off ground
- Balance on your two hands only (bipod)
- Tip back to squat

4. Tripod balance to Bipod balance

5. Tripod balance to tucked Headstand to straight Headstand balance

From tripod balance, lift hips upward so you can bring both knees together.

6. Bipod to Tripod to tucked Headstand to straight Headstand

7. Bipod to Tripod to tucked Headstand to straight Headstand - return to Bipod

Bipod to Headstand

Long sequence

Headstand back to Bipod

BALANCES ON THE HANDS

Handstands are also very good for developing both physical and motor qualities (strength, balance, spatial orientation),and, if appropriate progressions and safe practices are followed, can be taught to most age groups and ability levels.

Handstands are fundamental to most gymnastics sports and can develop excellent upper body strength in those sports in which they are not regularly performed (Trampoline, Rhythmics)

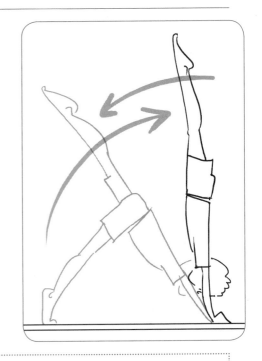

Safe teaching order

Safe Teaching Order

Use a developmentally sound teaching sequence. Here are the steps.

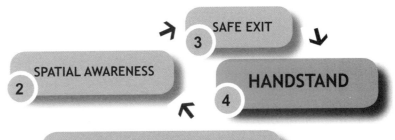

1. ARM + SHOULDER STRENGTH
2. SPATIAL AWARENESS
3. SAFE EXIT
4. HANDSTAND

1. First develop arm and shoulder strength and spatial awareness

It is very easy to perform partial or semi Handstands whereby the hands are placed on a mat and, with feet together, jump hips upwards to ½ handstand.

This is safer than kicking with 1 leg at a time because the gymnast may kick too hard and go right to a handstand and fall over.

Perform these semi handstands often to develop both strength and spatial awareness.

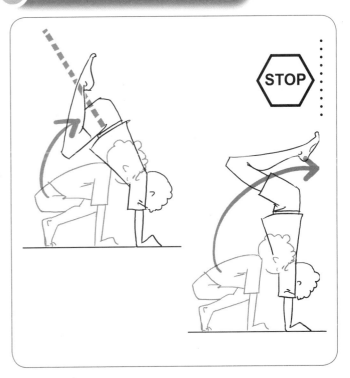

2. Develop 'turn-and-step-down' safe exit BEFORE EVER ARRIVING IN THE HANDSTAND.

Handstands in Review

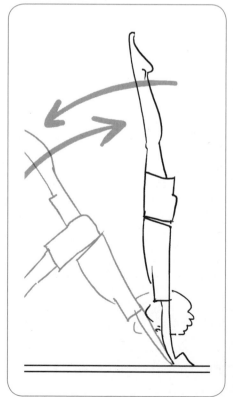

HANDSTANDS

It is very VERY important to teach gymnasts how to exit safely from a handstand BEFORE allowing them to perform a handstand.

Safe Exit Drills

Individually practise the following 'safe exit' drill for learning a Handstand:

- Kick (lift) 1 leg up to near handstand, and repeat several times.
- Kick (lift)1 leg to near handstand, then do ¼ turn on hands and step 1 arm forward.
- After completing step with hand, step 1 leg down from handstand.
- Repeat several times.
- Repeat several more times to the opposite side (1/4 turn opposite direction & step other hand).
- When, and only when, gymnasts can perform this safe exit, should they be allowed to go to a full handstand.

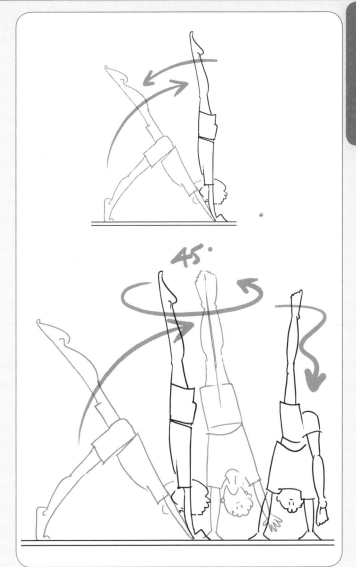

SAFETY
Even after learners have been doing full handstands for some time, they should still be instructed to regularly practise this safe exit drill.

Safe Entrance Drill with a Partner

With a partner, practise the following 'safe entrances' for learning a Handstand:

- Place 1 foot on box top or stack of mats (waist-high) and lift other leg gently to handstand
- Face away from a wall, do front support and walk feet up wall toward handstand
- Walk hands back toward wall until near handstand is reached.

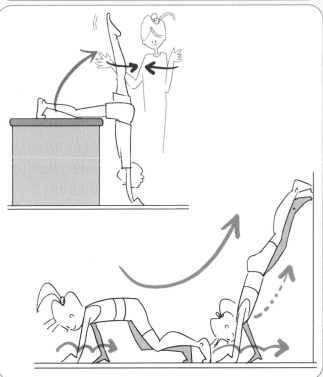

PARTNER BALANCES

In groups of 3, each coaches the other 2 in one of the following (#1- #3 below):

1. Coach partner chest balance

- Partner on hands and knees, other partner does tucked chest balance on back.
- You can grasp partner's arm and leg as you place your chest on her back.
- Or, you can reach 2 hands under and grasp his chest.

2. Coach partner knee balance

- One partner sits on bench or box top
- The other partner grasps that partner's hands in a double hand grasp
- Then steps onto the knees of the sitting partner ...
- And slowly leans backward as the sitting partner raises to a semi stand.

3. Coach partner back support

- Partners sit close, facing each other
- Raise legs up so feet are touching, and then
- Attempt to raise themselves off the ground so they are in support on hands, feet touching, hips off ground.

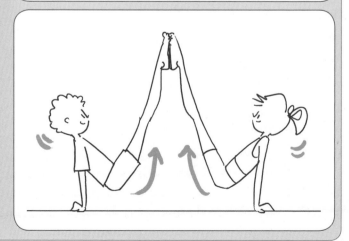

YOUR COACHING TASK

In groups of 4, each coaches the other 3 on one of the following (#1- #4 below).

BALANCES USING BALANCE BEAMS

1. Coach knee balances

Coach a variety of balances on knees and on hands and knees on beams, benches, box-tops etc.

2. Coach hip balances

Coach a variety of balances on hips (crossways and lengthways) on beam.

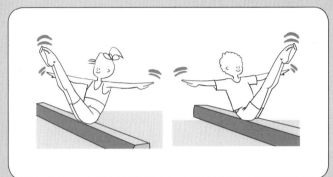

BALANCE WITH BALLS

3. Balance on body parts with balls

While balancing on body parts (feet, knees, shoulders) also balance a ball on some body part (on open hand, on the back of neck, between calves, etc).

4. 'Ball-ance' on body parts and on balls

Using balls of different sizes, balance on the balls:

- Both feet balancing on ball while holding front support.
- Both hands on ball while holding front support.

BASIC HANGS

Hanging is the third category of STATIONARY POSITIONS. These are the most stable of all because the Centre of Mass is suspended below the base.

Imagine standing on a horizontal bar (Balance), then doing front hip support (Support), then doing a long hang (Hang). Can you imagine how they become progressively more stable?

Describe how balances, supports and hangs are mechanically very different?

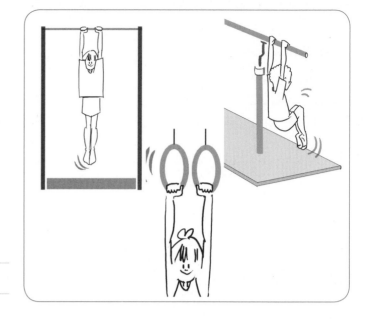

Where Do We Find Hanging Activities?

In some gymnastics sports there are no hanging activities (Trampoline, Rhythmic) and in some there is limited opportunity to hang when doing group activities (Aerobics, Acrobatics) while in Men's and Women's Artistic Gymnastics there is a lot of hanging activities both in STATIONARY POSITIONS and in SWING.

In recreational and educational gymnastics classes HANGING activities are extremely valuable for developing physical and motor qualities (FITNESS)

There is an obvious benefit for all gymnasts in all gymnastics sports to have opportunities to do hanging activities.

List some of the benefits you can gain by doing hanging activities?

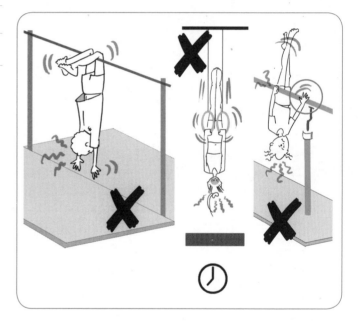

SAFETY
• Do not do inverted hangs from the knees only. This hang does little to increase strength, endurance or flexibility and has the potential for injury.
• Do not have gymnasts hang in inverted positions for long periods of time.
• Do not have gymnasts change hand grasps while inverted.

BASIC HANGS

Long Hangs

Hanging by the hands is safe and it enhances physical qualities such as grip strength, shoulder strength and shoulder flexibility. It can also enhance strength around other joints by doing the activities below.

Vary hand grasps

- Overgrasp
- Undergrasp
- Mixed grasp
- Crossed grasp

Vary leg positions

- Tuck
- Straddle
- Stride
- Pike

Vary arm positions

- Narrow grasp - straight arms
- Wide grasp - straight arms
- Narrow grasp - bent arms
- Wide grasp - bent arms

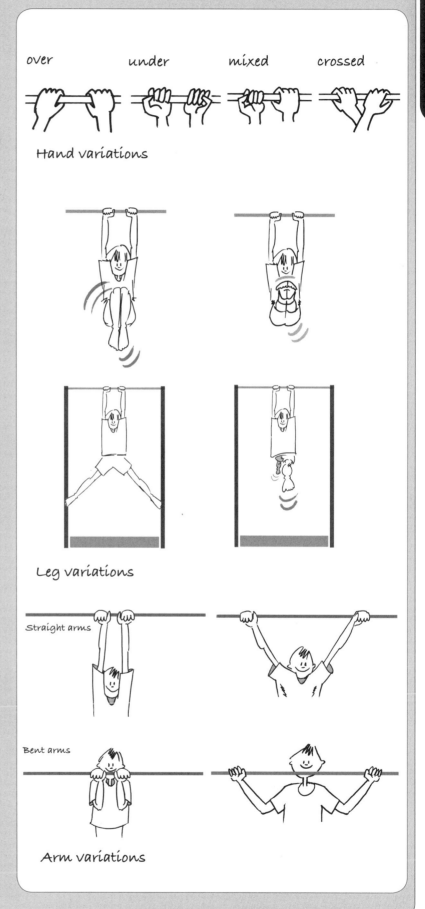

over   under   mixed   crossed

Hand variations

Leg variations

Straight arms

Bent arms

Arm variations

BASIC HANGS

Long Hang Activities for Young Athletes

- Hang in different Shapes (round, short, long, crooked)

- Letters (C, L, J, X, upside down V)

- Actions (wiggling, bicycling, pumping legs, corkscrewing, washing machine)

- Group of 3 or 4 hanging, pass the object with your feet (cube, hoop, bean bag).

- Each person makes a shape and rest have to copy.

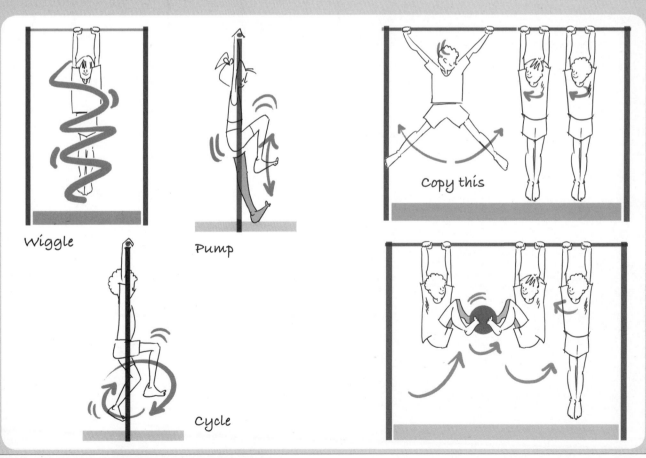

Wiggle

Pump

Cycle

Copy this

8

Landings

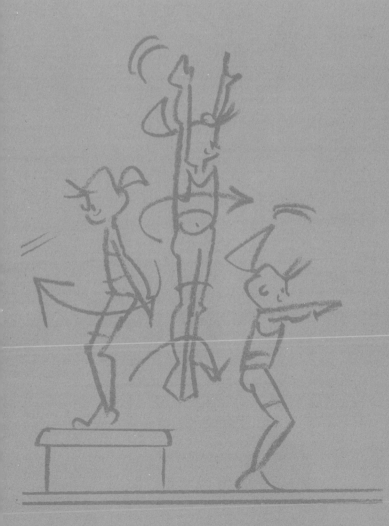

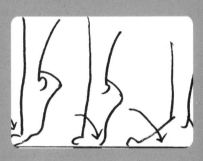

LANDINGS

MECHANICS OF LANDINGS

LANDINGS occur many times in all gymnastic sports. In some competitive events, LANDINGS occur when the routine terminates as a dismount. In other competitive events there are a series of LANDINGS throughout the routine. By far the greatest number of LANDINGS occur, however, during training and during gymnastics classes. And guess where almost all gymnastics injuries occur? Some occur on takeoffs — but most occur on LANDINGS.

℗ | Complete   Q14, 15 & 16

For 'LANDING' think 'absorbing force'.

LANDING and deceleration

When answering the previous 3 questions coaches often say: "slowly bending your legs will result in a safe LANDING". It is obvious that we must 'decelerate' the body in all LANDINGS and the slower we decelerate, the safer the LANDING. When LANDING on your feet, use your ankle, knee and hip muscles to decelerate slowly thereby absorbing the force of the LANDING.

Force absorption graphs

Let's look at a graph of the force absorption during LANDING. On the vertical axis we have the magnitude of the force of LANDING. On the horizontal axis we have the time it takes from the moment of contact with the ground until you have decelerated to 0 (you have absorbed all the LANDING force).

If you were to LAND very rigid (stiff kneed) the force would spike and look like the top diagram. If you were to slowly bend your knees and hips, the deceleration would be much slower (the force would be absorbed over a greater time period) and it would look like the bottom diagram.

✔ Decelerate slowly

✔ Use ankle | thigh | hip to cushion

✔ Aim for a 'flat' force diagram

Muscle contractions during LANDINGS

Example 1

Imagine 2 partners, 1 'piggy-back' on the other. The base (bottom) partner raises the heels off the floor. Can you see that the calf muscles are working 'positively' during the upward phase? They are contracting and shortening each time the heels raise.

The opposite occurs on the downward (heel lowering) phase. The calf muscles are working 'negatively' as the heels lower. They are lengthening in a braking function. In other words, they are decelerating the heel drop.

The upward or positive phase is called a concentric contraction (muscles are shortening), while the negative phase is called an eccentric contraction (muscles are lengthening - though still actively contracting).

This controlled 'deceleration' is the essence of all safe LANDINGS (also occurring at the knees and hips).

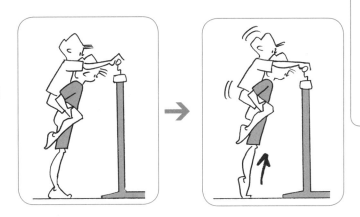

✔ Concentric | heels raise | muscles shorten

✔ Eccentric | heels lower | muscles lengthen

✔ In both cases the muscles are - contracting

Example 2

Another example of this braking (limb deceleration) LANDING action occurs when you 'kill' your bounce on Trampoline.

How many ways can we land?

	on the FEET	on the HANDS	with shoulder ROLLS
Forward			
Backward			
Sideward			

LANDING ON THE FEET

When LANDING on the feet, you have muscles crossing several anatomical joints that can decelerate the body (absorb the force of the LANDING)- the joints of the foot, ankles, knees and hips.

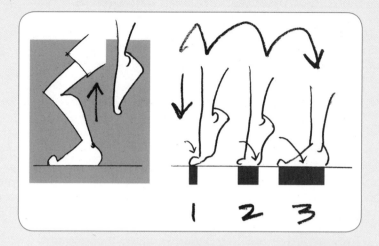

1. Decelerating - using foot/ankle joints

Perform a small jump upwards and LAND with straight knees so that you decelerate by using only the joints in the foot and ankle. Practise this sequential LANDING several times:

- Land on toes
- Then lower to the balls of the foot
- Then lower slowly to the heels
- You will soon be able to LAND softly and safely with straight legs from a small vertical jump starting in a standing position. Do not try this from an elevated surface.

SAFETY

We do not want you to LAND with straight legs any other time. This small LANDING with straight legs is an exercise to teach you that there is considerable deceleration in the feet and ankles.

In all subsequent LANDINGS on the feet you will first decelerate using the feet and ankles and immediately you will also bend the knees and hips to decelerate slowly.

2. Decelerating using the knee joints

Immediately after the heels lower to the ground, the knees slowly bend. That is, the Quadriceps muscles eccentrically contract so that knee flexion occurs slowly and the knee joints brake (decelerate) the LANDING.

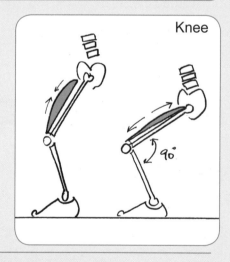

Knee

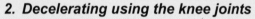

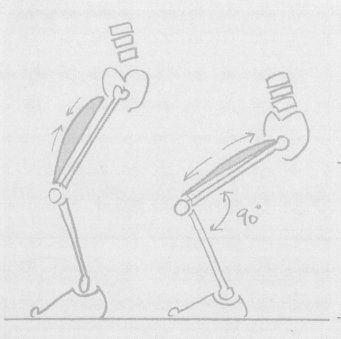

Landings on the feet

- ✔ First decelerate using the feet
- ✔ Immediately bend - ankles, knees and hips
- ✔ RESULT: a slow deceleration

3. Practise decelerating using the hip joints

At the same time the Quadriceps muscles decelerate knee flexion, the Gluteal muscles decelerate bending (flexing) about the hip joint.

Note that these two groups of muscles are the same ones that accelerate you upwards in springs. In springs they are contracting concentrically (shortening).

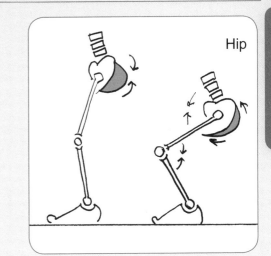

Hip

4. Practise lowering the arms

Another way to mechanically assist in reducing the force of the LANDING is to quickly lower the arms from overhead to horizontal as foot contact is made with the ground. This arm action reduces the force on the feet and at the same time stabilizes the LANDING.

The mechanical understanding of this will be explained in later courses.

5. Practise LANDING on the feet backward

Practise landing on your feet backward from various elevated surfaces.

LANDING ON THE FEET SIDEWARD

Generally, LANDING sideward from high heights (as in dismounts from apparatus or from vaults) is discouraged in Artistic Gymnastics because of the possibility of knee damage.

There are many instances where gymnasts will LAND sideward in Rhythmic Gymnastics, Aerobic Gymnastics, and the dance portion of floor exercises in Artistic Gymnastics. It is prudent we teach children how to safely LAND sideward while at the same time discouraging LANDING sideward from dismounts and vaults.

LANDING ON FEET FORWARD

Activity 1 - Landing from a small height

Go with a partner to different elevated surfaces and practise:

- Observe and correct each other
- Look for efficient deceleration at each joint
- Listen for quiet LANDING
- Look for arm movement downward

Activity 2 - Landing after shaped jump

Make different shapes in the air as you jump down:

- Star, tuck (knees together and knees apart)
- Straddle
- Pike
- One leg tucked, the other piked
- Can you think of a different shape?
- Observe and correct partner's LANDING

Activity 3 - Landing from higher heights

Go with partner to progressively higher elevated surfaces and practise LANDINGS:

- Observe and correct each other

✔ Quiet LANDINGS
✔ Move arms downward

Activity 4 - Landing after jump ½ turn

Jump backward and do a ½ turn to LAND forward on the feet:

- Do this from low heights first and progress to higher heights only when your partner is satisfied you are proficient at the low heights
- Observe and correct each other

Coaching LANDING

Activity 5 - Land forward

In groups of 4, each person has a
number.

- Number 1 teaches and corrects
  the group on the basics of how
  to LAND on the feet forward
- Number 2 then teaches and
  corrects the group on how to
  LAND from low heights and
  making different shapes in the
  air
- Number 3 then teaches and
  corrects the group on how to
  LAND from higher heights
- Number 4 then teaches and
  corrects the group on how
  to jump backward, do a ½ turn and LAND
  forward (from low, medium and finally, higher
  heights)

LANDING on feet backward & sideward

Repeat Activities 1, 2, 3, and 4 above using
backward LANDINGS.

SAFETY

Using 'fat' mats does not teach good
LANDING technique and injuries may occur
getting off them.

GAMES TO TEACH LANDING ON THE FEET

1. Follow-the-leader

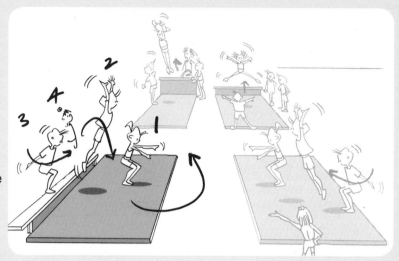

- Groups of 4 participants with 1 designated as the first 'leader'.
- The leader proceeds to run to various 'elevated stations' and perform a different LANDING on the feet from each station.
- The rest of the group follows and copies the same LANDING.
- After a short time, the next gymnast in the group will become the new leader.
- Repeat until all 4 have been leader.

2. Starburst and Stick Landing

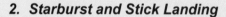

- Groups of 4, each group standing on an elevated surface, all participants facing a different direction.
- On signal, all jump together (in different directions) and perform the designated LANDING and try to 'stick'.
- Repeat several times before all groups rotate to different elevated surface and repeat using different LANDING on the feet.

3. Space Docking Tag

- Group random running around the gym containing several elevated surfaces with 2 or more designated chasers.
- If caught by a chaser, you exchange places with chaser after performing 2 jump ½ turns with good LANDING.
- You are 'immune' from being tagged if 'docked' on an elevated surface.
- Only 1 person can be 'docked' at a time on each "space station".
- If anyone else jumps onto the station, the person on the station must jump off and LAND correctly before running.
- Same LANDING will be done by all, and will change as the game progresses.

LANDING ON THE HANDS

Ⓠ | Complete   Q17

Forward

Backward

Sideward

LANDING on the hands forward

When LANDING on the hands, we have the muscle crossing several anatomical joints that can decelerate the body (absorb the force of the LANDING) - the joints of the hand and wrists, the elbows and the shoulders.

Decelerating using hands and wrists

If you do a front support and move up onto your fingers, then down onto your hands you can feel how you decelerate using:

- First the fingers
- Then lower to the palm of the hand,
- Then lower slowly to the heel of the hand

In all subsequent LANDINGS on the hands you will first decelerate using the hands and wrists and immediately you will also bend the elbows and shoulders to decelerate slowly.

Decelerating using elbows & shoulders

The eccentric contraction of the shoulder muscles (Deltoids) and elbow muscles (Triceps) decelerate the body.

Triceps

Deltoids

SAFETY
LANDING on the hands is NOT recommended on trampolines or in a pit.

LANDING on the hands backward

Falling backward on an outstretched arm is a frequent cause of wrist or elbow injury in the general population. It is the natural reflex to reach back with your hands (fingers pointing away from your body) when you slip or fall backward. Unfortunately this position of the hand (fingers facing backward) locks the elbow and you are unable to bend your arms to decelerate the fall.

If, instead, you turn your hand so that the fingers are facing towards the body then you are able to bend the elbow and thus use Triceps muscles to decelerate the bending of the elbow and LAND safely.

Decelerating using hands & wrists

If you squat and fall backward onto your hands you can decelerate completely by just using the muscles of the hand and wrist. That is, you can decelerate using:

- First the fingers
- Then lower to the palm of the hand,
- Then lower slowly to the heel of the hand

Decelerating using elbows & shoulders

The eccentric contraction of the shoulder muscles (Deltoids) and elbow muscles (Triceps) decelerate the body. As you lower your seat to the ground, you can continue decelerating by rolling on your back.

LANDING ON THE HANDS FORWARD

Individually practise LANDING softly and quietly while falling forward onto your hands. Use the following sequence:

- From kneeling
- From a wide straddle stand
- From progressively narrower straddle stands
- Eventually from a stand with feet together

LANDING on the feet forward, then LANDING on the hands forward

Individually practise LANDING on your feet forward from elevated surfaces and then immediately fall forward and LAND forward on your hands:

- From knee height
- From waist height
- From waist height with a jump

Jump backward with ½ turn to land forward on feet then fall forward onto your hands.

- From knee height
- From waist height
- From waist height with a jump

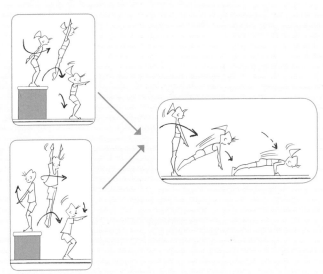

LANDING ON THE HANDS BACKWARD

Preparation

In a sitting position on the floor or mats, place your hands on the floor behind you (fingers pointing away from body) and experience how this locks the elbows.

Now turn your hands so that your fingers point towards the body (fingers facing forward). You will see that you are now able to bend your elbows.

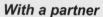
Individually, practise the following:

- From a squat, with fingers pointing forward, fall backward onto your hands and finish in a bent knee sit
- Use your wrist and elbow joints to decelerate as you fall from a squat to a bent-knee sit
- Practise this several times
- Now, from a squat, fall backward onto the hands (fingers pointing forward) and roll to your shoulders
- Practise this several times

With a partner

Progressively increase the height you are falling from.

Take turns so that both you and your partner are checking that your fingers are pointing forward before you fall:

- First, from a full squat,
- Then, if above is efficient, do from a ¾ squat,
- Then, if above is efficient, do from a ½ squat,
- Then, if above is efficient, do from a ¼ squat.

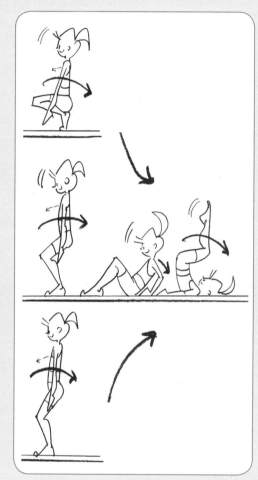

SAFETY
• Fingers face towards the body • Allow the elbow to safely bend • Cushion the landing

LANDING on the feet backward, then LANDING on hands backward

Individually practise LANDING on your feet backward from elevated surfaces and then immediately fall backward and LAND backward on your hands:

- From knee height
- From waist height

LANDING ON THE HANDS BACKWARD

Coach Landing on the Hands

In groups of 3, take a turn teaching the others LANDING on hands forward and backward.

- Group provides feedback
- Each of the 3 participants in 1 of the groups will teach the whole class a LANDING game from the 3 following games.

In groups of 3, take a turn teaching the others

LANDING on the hands backward

1. Forward counter balancing

- Divide group into pairs that are size matched. Pairs stand back to back and hold hands.
- Partners slowly lean forward until they are counter balanced with straight arms.
- On signal from one partner, both release their hands and fall forward to land on hands.

As always, participants can choose a starting position (legs together or straddled) that is comfortable for them to fall forward from.

2. *Dominoes*

- Line up a group of 6 to 10 participants with toes against edge of a mat.

  Since they are going to LAND forward on their hands they will want to assume a starting position that they are comfortable with (legs together or legs straddled to lower themselves closer to mat).

- On your signal, the first participant will fall forward to LAND on hands, and then sequentially, each participant will do the same in a falling dominoes effect.

- Practise several times to get good domino effect.

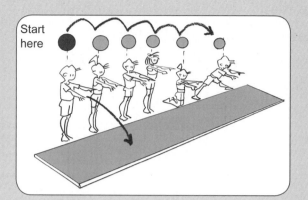

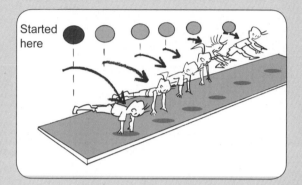

Variations

Start from one end
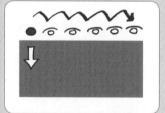

Start from the opposite end
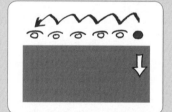

Start from middle, proceed left & right
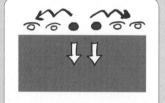

Start on opposite sides of mat
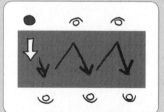

Alternate direction participants are facing
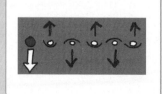

3. Backward counter-balance

Preparation

Before doing this activity, review and practice LANDING backward on the hands.

- Pairs stand front to front and hold hands.

- Partners slowly lean backward until they are counter balanced with straight arms.

- On signal from one partner, both release their hands and fall backward to LAND on hands.

- As always, participants can choose a starting position (legs straight or bent) that is comfortable for them to fall backward from.

4. Timber tag

What to do

- Class runs randomly, with 2 or more participants designated (arm raised or carrying scarf etc.) as the chasers.

- When chasers tag another participant, the tagged gymnast stops, yells out 'timber' and LANDS forward on the hands from a comfortable starting position.

- The chaser is now 'free' and the tagged gymnast becomes a new 'chaser'.

LANDING WITH SHOULDER ROLLS

Ⓠ | Complete Q18 & 19

Forward	
Backward	
Sideward	

The following shoulder rolls are quite difficult and require expert instruction and diligent practise before you are competent to perform and teach. You will be guided carefully.

These LANDINGS are very important life skills as well as gymnastics skills and may very well save you from serious injury outside gymnastics. The rolls that we do for safety LANDINGS are not the same as the rolls we do at other times in gymnastics sports.

Since our goal in LANDINGS is to decelerate the body safely, we will always protect our head and neck by moving them out of harms way. We want the head to avoid contact during safety rolls therefore we will always perform shoulder rolls (we do NOT want to increase body surface area by banging our head on the floor).

Force dissipation

✓ use as many joints as possible

✓ bend them as slowly as possible

Principle 1 - Force Dissipation

We have been discussing a general mechanical principle that is the basis for all safe LANDINGS. What is it?

To reduce the impact of any LANDING, we slowly absorb (or dissipate) the LANDING force. In other words, we decelerate safely by using as many joints as possible and bending them as slowly as possible.

Maximize surface area

✔ The landing forces are 'dissipated' over the maximum surface area.

Principle 2 - Maximize Body Surface Area

There is another general mechanical principle that is utilized in many safe LANDINGS: Dissipate the force of a LANDING over as much body surface area as possible.

This mechanical principle is utilized when we do rolls when LANDING. That is, if we have too much linear velocity to LAND safely on our hands or feet, then we dissipate the force over more time and more body surface by rolling.

Imagine running quickly in a gym and then tripping and falling forward onto your hands. You would skid across the floor on your hands and chest (and that would not be much fun).

LANDING WITH SHOULDER ROLLS

The task

You will be taught 3 different LANDINGS with rolls.
Later you will be assigned to groups of 3.
Each group will teach 1 of these skills to other
coaches or to demonstration groups.
Everyone will have a chance to observe and
correct.

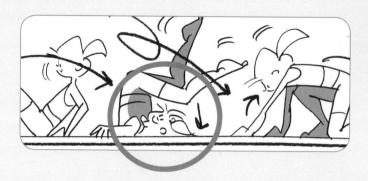

Backward Shoulder Roll

Since this is the easiest safety roll to learn, we will
do it first. Most people can perform this with very
little instruction.

Activity 1

* From squat, sit and roll backward over 1 shoulder to land on 1 or 2 knees.

* If you have difficulty, extend 1 arm sideward (i.e. if rolling over left shoulder, extend left arm along the ground sideward).

* If still having difficulty, you may want to roll down a slight decline (wedge mat).

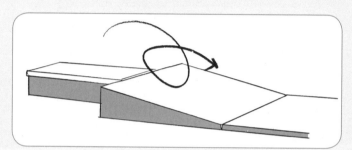

✓ Checklist

* Hands correct?
* Head position correct?

* Each student checks the other 2 in your group to see that the head is turning to the same side as the roll.

* If you are rolling over your left shoulder, your head should be turned to the left (thus eyes are looking at the knees touching down).

* If you are looking in the opposite direction it can be a bit stressful on the neck.

* Repeat the backward shoulder roll several times to each side (right and left).

SIDEWARD SHOULDER ROLL

Activity 1

Full side roll

- Start on your hands and knees.
- Do a full roll sideways to finish on your hands and knees again (barrel roll).
- Do this to the left and to the right. You can also do this down a slight decline.

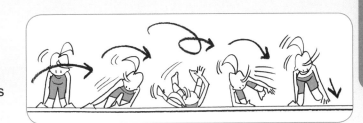

Activity 2

'Hug a barrel'

- Start on hands and knees and
- Make yourself more 'barrel' shaped by turning your hands inward, 1 hand on top of the other hand
- The bottom hand determines the direction of the roll (left hand on bottom if rolling to the left) and bending the elbows slightly (as if you were hugging a small barrel).
- Roll to the left and to the right several times while trying to maintain the barrel shape throughout the roll.

Activity 3

Shoulder roll from lunge

- Perform the barrel roll from a starting position of a deep lunge to the right and a deep lunge to the left
- It is normal to perform the roll only across the upper back and shoulders at this stage
- Observe and correct each other as you try to maintain the same arm shape throughout the roll.

✔ *Checklist*

- Hands turned inward
- 1 hand on top of the other
- Bottom hand determines the direction of the roll.

Remember

✔ Use a large area to dissipate the LANDING forces

✔ Maintain 'barrel arms'

Activity 4

Roll down a decline

Make the roll easier by trying rolling down a slight decline.

- Take 1 or 2 steps into the roll -
  (maintain barrel shape during roll
  1 hand is on top of the other)
- Kick the leading leg fairly aggressively -
  (you need momentum, so push hard into the roll)

Activity 5

Finishing position

- From shoulder balance, roll forward
- Bend your left leg and roll onto left knee, right foot

- From shoulder balance, roll forward
- Bend your right knee and roll onto right knee, left foot

- Do sideward shoulder roll to the right
- Finish on your left knee and right foot

- Do sideward shoulder roll to the left
- Finish on your right knee and left foot

Note

Using a sloped surface (decline) is very useful in learning forward shoulder rolls (such as a wedge shaped mat or a beat board with mat on top).

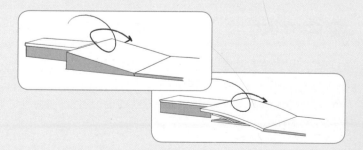

FORWARD SHOULDER ROLL

Below are several activities that teach how to dissipate the landing forces over the hands, arms and shoulders, then along the entire surface area of the back and hips.

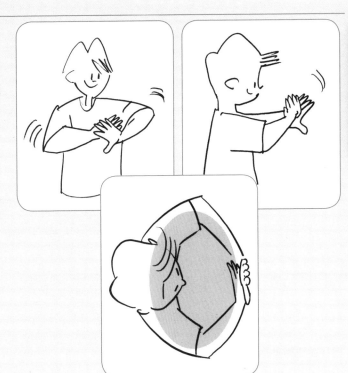

1. Make a barrel

While standing, make a barrel shape with your arms, with 1 hand on top of the other and bend your elbows slightly as if you are hugging a small barrel.

2. Maintain the barrel

Below are activities to help you develop the strength to support your body weight during the roll - key requirement of successful shoulder rolls.

- Hold a front support with arms in barrel shape.
- Try to do 1/4 push ups in this position (you may have to support on hands and knees to do this)

Stand and face a partner
so that both of you have hands forward in barrel position. Resist pushing each other backward while maintaining the barrel shape.

As with sideward shoulder rolls, the bottom hand will determine the direction of the roll. If the left hand is on the bottom, you will be rolling over your left shoulder.

3. Diagonally Position the Arms

In order to position our arms to help dissipate the force of a forward shoulder roll we must change them from a horizontal position in front of us, to a diagonal position.

4. *Forward shoulder roll using a decline*

Now you are ready to begin rolling. It is much easier to learn it down a decline and with some forward momentum.

- Do a forward roll but with your hands in the tilted barrel position
- Progressively move your head more and more to the side so your head does not touch the mat as you roll
- Roll to your feet
- If you are rolling over your left shoulder, you will be looking to the right and vice versa. Do not let your arms bend more than the 'barrel' position.
- Practise to both sides

Once perfected on decline, practise on flat surface.

Make it easier with a decline

Dissipating the landing forces

✔ ensure contact with hands, arms, shoulders, back & hips

✔ maintain the barrel position

5. *Finishing off*

As with the sideward shoulder roll you need to finish the forward shoulder roll in a comfortable and efficient position, usually with the leading leg bent so that you finish on that knee and the other foot.

LANDING WITH SHOULDER ROLLS

Organization - In groups of 3, each participant takes a turn coaching their assigned shoulder roll to the other 2.

At the conclusion of instruction, the 2 'gymnasts' will give feedback to the 'coach'.

You should clearly explain how the technique 'satisfies' the mechanical principles (dissipate force over time and body surface).

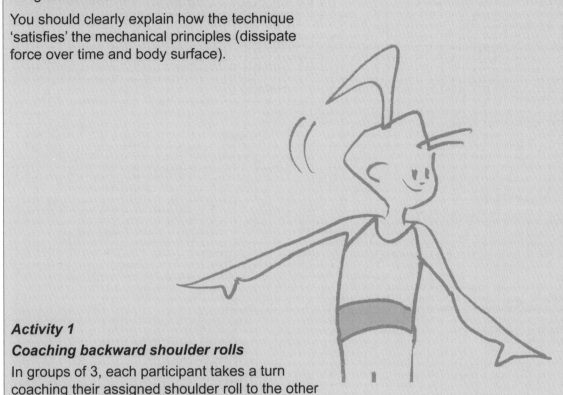

Activity 1

Coaching backward shoulder rolls

In groups of 3, each participant takes a turn coaching their assigned shoulder roll to the other two.

At the conclusion of instruction, the 2 'gymnasts' will give feedback to the 'coach'.

You should clearly demonstrate how the technique 'satisfies' the mechanical principles (dissipate force over time and body surface).

Activity 1

Landing with shoulder rolls - continued

Activity 2

Coaching sideward shoulder rolls

In groups of 3, each participant takes a turn coaching their assigned shoulder roll to the other two.

At the conclusion of instruction, the 2 'gymnasts' will give feedback to the 'coach'.

You should clearly demonstrate how the technique 'satisfies' the mechanical principles (dissipate force over time and body surface).

Activity 2

Activity 2

Activity 3

Coaching forward shoulder rolls

In groups of 3, each participant takes a turn coaching their assigned shoulder roll to the other two.

At the conclusion of instruction, the 2 'gymnasts' will give feedback to the 'coach'.

You should clearly demonstrate how the technique 'satisfies' the mechanical principles (dissipate force over time and body surface).

Activity 3

Teaching & Learning

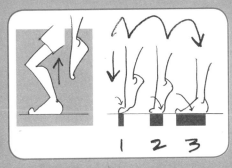

TEACHING AND LEARNING

Do you recall our educational philosophy?

THE LEARNING PROCESS

Learning can be thought of as 'a relatively permanent change that is the result of experience'.

Learners experience through their senses and in the case of learning physical and motor skills the main senses are:

Visual

Tactile

Auditory · Receiving & processing verbal instruction

Kinesthetic · Both proprioceptive and vestibular

Let's first examine how we acquire and retain cognitive skills then look at physical and motor skills acquisition.

Once we become aware of new cognitive learning material via our senses, we must then commit it to memory. As it turns out, memory is a complex array of neural currents and is divided into short term, medium term & long term memory.

In order to move from short term to long-term memory we must engage various strategies to create a memory trail. Mostly this is done by repetition, but of course other retention techniques such as mnemonics are also useful.

Is it the same with learning physical skills? Not exactly, but similar.

What is your learning style?

First your senses must be alerted to what is to be learned. A verbal description (auditory), a picture or a demonstration (visual), or having your body moved through the actual skill (kinesthetic).

Some people learn more readily with one type of sensory input than with others, but all physical skill acquisition follows the same learning journey. That is, we all pass through the same phases:

FITTS 3 STAGES OF LEARNING PHYSICAL SKILLS

The Cognitive (Understanding) Phase

- Getting the "feel" of a skill
- Trial and error, eliminate incorrect responses
- Do not over-teach, do not over-verbalize
- Gymnast has many cues and responses that later will be automatic

The Intermediate Phase

Noticeable learning takes place

- Errors are gradually being eliminated, performance more consistent
- Models important at this stage
- Verbalization = via key words

The Automatic Phase

- Performance consistent and automatic
- Fine-tuning stage
- Specific parts of skill can be isolated for conscious improvement.

As a coach, you can enjoy watching students go through these stages with every new skill.

Factors That Facilitate Learning Physical Skills

- Physical (ESP&F) and motor (ABC'S) components that are well developed will aid learning.
- Practise bouts, repeated often, are more effective than lengthy practice sessions on a single skill.
- Material should be interesting and meaningful.
- Learning is fastest when gymnast is strongly motivated.
- Progress is more rapid when gymnast is often successful.
- Motor performance is enhanced in social context.
- Knowledge of Results (feedback) is very important

INTRODUCTION TO THE TEACHING PROCESS

More than one teaching style

There is a continuum of methods or 'styles' that teachers / coaches use to introduce sensory stimuli to learners. On one end of the continuum is the completely teacher-directed learning and on the other end of the continuum is the completely learner-directed learning.

Drills vs Movement Problems

The coach / teacher-directed style would include the use of specific drills and progressions for the learner, while a less coach-directed style would include giving students movement problems to solve on their own.

Efficiency vs Creativity

There are, of course, advantages and disadvantages to using different teaching styles.

Learning by way of drills and progressions can lead to correct and efficient learning of technique, but it can supress creativity and the realization of individual differences. Problem-solving learning styles would be the opposite.

Good teachers / coaches use a variety of teaching styles including the in-between styles that incorporate aspects of both ends of the continuum.

Combining methods - an example

An example would be guided discovery styles where the coach allows students to solve movement problems that are themselves carefully designed to guide the students to a desirable outcome while still allowing some room for creative solutions and individual differences.

Course note ...

In this course we will often use 'reciprocal teaching' whereby 2 partners teach each other and we will also use 'micro teaching' in very small groups. In each of these learning situations, you can practise using the more teacher-led styles or the more student-led styles.

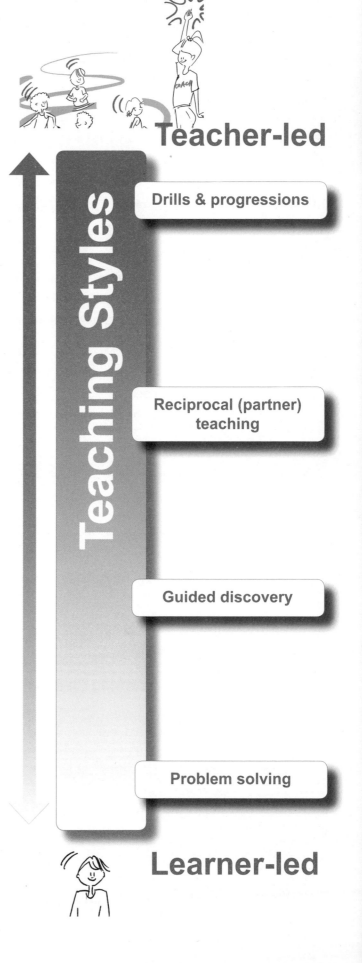

Teacher-led

Teaching Styles

Drills & progressions

Reciprocal (partner) teaching

Guided discovery

Problem solving

Learner-led

TO 'SPOT' OR NOT TO 'SPOT'

Spotting is the term used in gymnastics when one person physically catches or guides another person. At this stage of your coach education, you are not trained to spot gymnasts for safety, and if a skill needs to be spotted for a safety reason, the skill is inappropriate!

A coach at this level should not remedy a potentially dangerous situation by spotting. Instead, the potentially dangerous situation should be removed.

You Have Many Ways to Make Gymnastics Absolutely Safe:

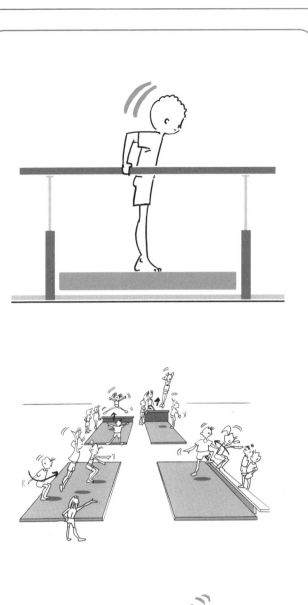

- Lower apparatus, or raise mats
- Provide more lead-up activities to a skill
- Better physical preparation of the gymnasts
- Disallow certain skills until the gymnasts are better prepared to learn the skills by themselves
- And of course, teach gymnasts to 'manage their own bodies' by teaching them to LAND efficiently and then continually practise LANDINGS every class.

Spotting and loss of focus

Another reason to eliminate spotting at the introductory levels is that if you are spotting one gymnast, you cannot be coaching the others in your group. This course and text will give you many suggestions as to how to teach introductory gymnastics without needing to spot gymnasts.

In the example opposite, the coach could ask the top gymnast to maintain a tucked position and very slowly straighten 1 leg at a time, and return to tuck as soon as the balance becomes unstable. In other words, teach the gymnasts to manage their own bodies rather than holding them on positions.

Course note ...

In subsequent courses you will be taught how to manually guide gymnasts to help with their learning. You will be given instruction in what is appropriate and what is inappropriate touching in gymnastics coaching. And in more advanced courses you will, of course, be taught how to spot gymnasts for both safety and learning.

TEACH MOVEMENT PATTERNS

It is important to point out that you are attempting to teach participants how to move in a gymnastics manner (FUNDAMENTALS). Learning individual skills is not as important as developing proficiency in learning:

- How to LAND safely (being indestructible)
- How to hold STATIONARY POSITIONS
- How to LOCOMOTE in gymnastics ways
- How to SPRING effectively from legs and arms
- How to ROTATE about all 3 axes

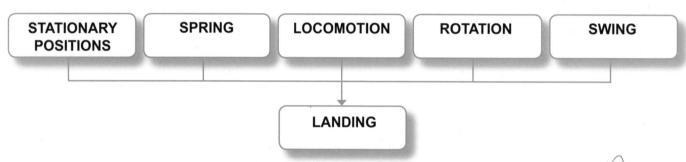

| STATIONARY POSITIONS | SPRING | LOCOMOTION | ROTATION | SWING |

LANDING

MOVING FROM THEORY TO PRACTICE

In addition to the preceding theory material on teaching and learning, the following information will be helpful for developing CLASS MANAGEMENT skills. As you can appreciate, it is difficult to teach anyone who is running wildly around the gym, or who is in deep conversation with another person, or who is in deep thought and is oblivious to your wonderful teaching!

Managing a group in a gymnastics setting can be a challenge, especially if the group consists of children full of energy and excitement. The energy and excitement, however, are also factors that make coaching so rewarding and so much fun.

The following are class management skills that will help you to channel the energy and excitement into FUN, FITNESS and FUNDAMENTALS.

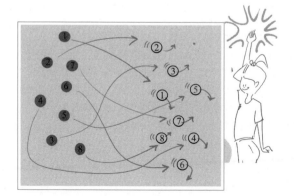

CLASS MANAGEMENT

1. Getting their Attention

- Sit the participants when you are addressing them
- Position yourself so that there is a wall behind you (thus you are the most interesting thing in their field of view)
- Speak slowly, clearly, concisely but be animated
- Have efficient 'stopping' signals such as:
- Raise your arm, they stop and raise their arm
    - *Yell "look sharp", they stop, hold hands together over their head*
    - *Yell "hit the deck", they drop onto their stomachs*

2. Herding the Wee Ones

- "Follow me" (group walking, running behind you)
- Group running (circles, random, shapes, etc.)
- "Toes to that line" or "toes to the edge of that mat"
- "All touch so and so and sit down"
- "All touch that blue mat and sit down"
- "All put 1 foot (hand) in that hoop, or on that mat"
- "Line up behind me, or ... behind so and so"
- "Everybody sit facing a partner"
- Ideas from the group….

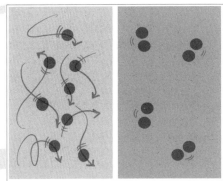

3. Getting Class Into Groups

- Play the game "communities" by calling out a number and have the class quickly sit in groups of that number.
- To get a group into a circle it is quickest if the participants join hands to make the circle
- To get the group into a line it is best to have them line-up with their toes against a mat, or toes to a line.

Complete Q20

MAXIMIZE PARTICIPATION IN GYM CLASS

1. Taking attendance - better practices

- Pre-arrange class into pairs - take absenteeism by asking single person who their missing partner is.
- Self-administered attendance upon entry to gym (discs, cards, sheet)
- Numbers on wall or floor, gymnast covers his/her number at some designated time in class. Take attendance by noting the uncovered number.
- More ideas from the group?

2. Warm-up stretching – better practices

Stretching at the very beginning of a recreational class is a time waster and ineffective since it is only done once or twice a week (and it certainly is not fun for the participants).

- Play a game that warms up the class and also provides stretching of joints (warm up should set mood / tone of class and slow stretching is a poor way to start).
- Do some stretching during rotations or at stations to reduce time wasted in line-ups.
- Do some stretching at a specific time after the class has warmed up with games.

3. Waiting for a 'turn' – better practices

This is the biggest single activity waster in gym classes.

- Delay the return to line-ups by doing some constructive activity such as practising a SPRING activity or a LOCOMOTION activity.
- Work *across* mats and apparatus rather than *along* the mats or apparatus.
- Where it is safe, divide apparatus into sections and have participants work in a section.
- When waiting for turns, give participants some constructive tasks to practise.
- When waiting for hand apparatus or for their turn on trampoline, have students engaged in some constructive activity.
- Be imaginative in ways to prevent line-ups.

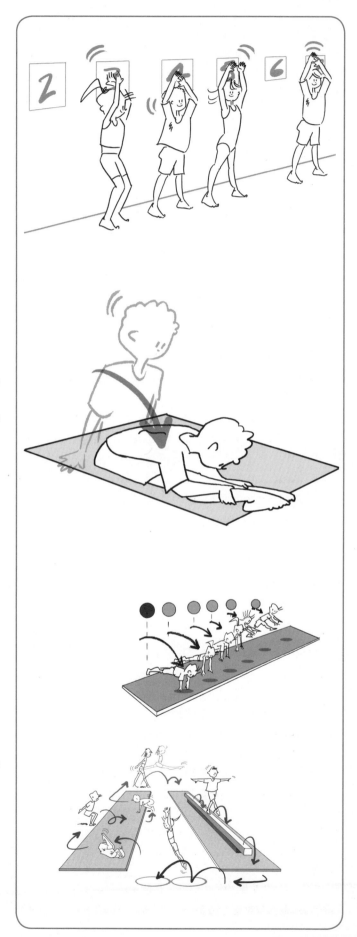

4. Changing stations - better practices

If your classes are set up so that participants change 'stations' several times during the class this can be a source of wasted time. The following are suggestions for making these transitions more active, more fun, and a beneficial part of the class:

- Points given to best group on each rotation, accumulate points
- "Move to next space station"
- "Move to next trough" (farm animal walks)
- "Move to next watering hole" (wild animal walks)
- "Move to next airport" (helicopters, planes)
- Always line-up in the same order (this eliminates much of the pushing and shoving)
- "Whole group move to the next station like ..."

Move like ...

1. A train, (hands on shoulders of person in front)
2. A train, (interlocking hoops)
3. A big bubble (join hands in a circle)
4. Little bubbles (join both hands of partner)
5. A giant jellyfish (join hands in a circle)
6. A hairy caterpillar (all holding rope, arms out)
7. A snowplow (side by side arms about waists)
8. A starfish (all holding on to a hoop)

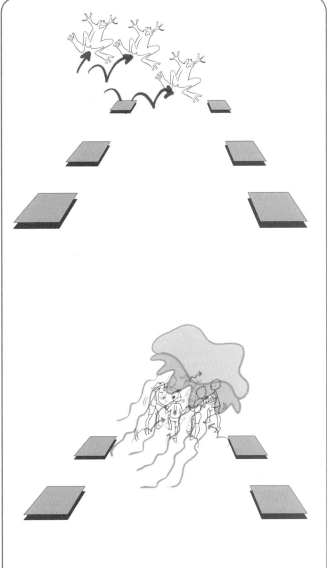

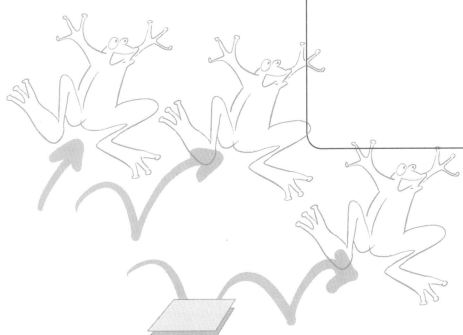

Wasting time gathering and moving equipment

Avoid wasting time collecting equipment such as balls, bean bags, hoops, clubs, etc.

Hand apparatus in containers (on wheels) in central location or at specific stations. Other ideas for hand apparatus efficiency?

1. Time savers

For gyms that have to set up and tear down gymnastics equipment here are some time savers:

- Specific group sets up or tears down specific apparatus every week
- Coaches come early to set up
- Outsiders hired (weight lifting club)
- Other suggestions from the group

2. Ideas for moving / storing equipment

- Use scooters under equipment to be moved
- Swivel wheels (casters) on all 4 corners of large mat or apparatus wagons
- Tape on chains for correct placement of cable hooks
- Chains hung in storage room
- Storage area painted for apparatus placement
- Use upper areas first (often top half of storage room is unused so build shelves or hang nets)

Other ideas to make equipment set up / tear down efficient?

....

....

....

....

....

....

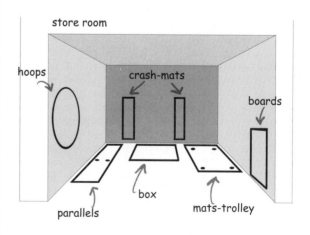

store room

hoops

crash-mats

boards

parallels

box

mats-trolley

10

Spring

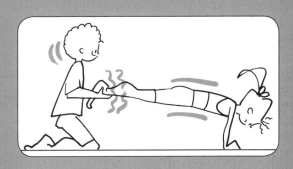

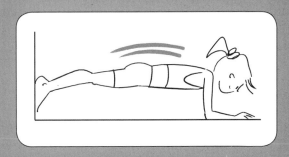

know this ...

SPRING

MECHANICS OF SPRING

Many gymnastics activities are the result of a single dynamic takeoff or spring. In Artistic Gymnastics, the vault and tumbling takeoffs from both the legs and the arms are examples of SPRING. The dance-type jumps, leaps and hops in Women's Artistic, Rhythmic Gymnastics and Aerobic Gymnastics are also SPRINGS, as are the rebounds (jumps) of Trampoline, Double Mini Trampoline and Tumbling.

SPRING can occur from 2 feet, 1 foot, 2 arms (rarely 1 arm) and from body parts on trampoline (SPRING from seat, SPRING from back (to ball out), SPRING from front (to cody), etc.).

GOOD SPRINGING FUNDAMENTALS

Good SPRING technique depends on 3 'mechanical' conditions:

1. Powerful muscles in the take-off limbs

Power is a combination of strength and speed Thus exercises should develop strength & speed in the take-off muscles.

2. A rigid body

Keeping a rigid body during any SPRING guarantees that the generated force is utilized in propelling the body. If the body is not rigid, the generated force will be 'absorbed' by the body.

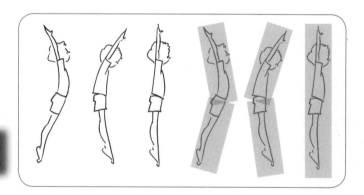

𝒬 | Complete   Q21 & 22

3. Use of non-support limb to increase force

Stand on a trampoline (or bathroom scale) & raise your arms quickly overhead. Your feet will be pressed down as your arms go up (action / reaction). Thus, when you are in contact with a SPRINGING device, moving your arms upward will increase the SPRING force.

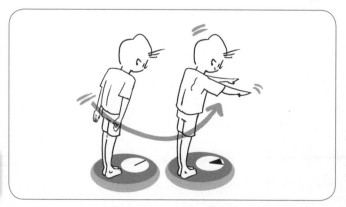

𝒬 | Complete   Q23

PHYSICAL PREPARATION FOR SPRING

We need to develop power in the gymnast's take-off limbs and develop rigid bodies in order to be efficient in any spring activity. This should be done using games, circuits and other enjoyable activities.

While doing spring activities and games we will not only be strengthening the gymnasts' take-off muscles, but we should also continually encourage gymnasts to maintain rigid trunks and hips. They can easily develop poor technique if they do not learn to coordinate the spring muscle contractions with the trunk stabilizing muscle contractions.

Exercises to Enhance Power:

In groups of 4, share ideas of games / activities that will develop leg power for 2 legged springing.

Keep in mind that you want to develop explosive actions - thus you are trying to selectively recruit fast twitch muscle fibres.

Note
Jumping in fat soft mats will be counter productive for developing explosive power.

Record your group's ideas.

Each group will demonstrate their top 2 ideas and you can record some of them below:

PHYSICAL PREPARATION FOR KEEPING A RIGID BODY

RIGID BODY ACTIVITIES

In pairs, follow instructions on exercises to enhance rigid body.

1. Banana rocking

- On your stomach (prone).
- On your back (supine).
- On your sides.

2. Banana rolling

- Start on your back with legs and shoulders off the mat (in-curve).
- Roll 180° to lie on stomach with legs and chest off the mat (outcurve).
- Repeat several times, without letting your upper body or legs touch the mat.

3. Rock and rolling

- Roll to side, rock 3 times.
- Roll to front, rock 3 times on front.

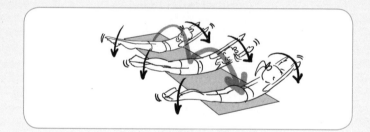

4. The plank

- Hold rigid, straight position, with calves and shoulders supported between 2 box tops.
- Push down gently on the centre of your partner's trunk so s/he has to resist.
- Repeat facing up, and facing down.
- Move the support boxes further and further apart.

try this ....

In pairs, follow instructions on exercises to enhance rigid body.

5. Lower the drawbridge

- Shoulder balance, reach back and grasp wall bars (or partner's ankles).
- Lower feet toward the floor, then return to shoulder balance.
- Repeat several times.
- Maintain a straight body position.

6. No saggy baggy

- While holding front support, partner pushes down gently on both hips.
- Gymnast in front support resists any sag in the trunk.
- Continue constant downward push, until lower partner says to stop.
- Repeat in back support.

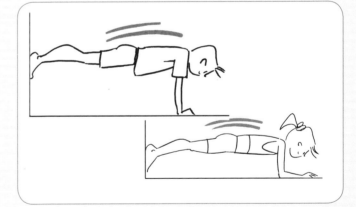

7. Wall supported front support

- Front support on hands, feet on wall - shoulder height.
- Front support on elbows, feet on wall - shoulder height.

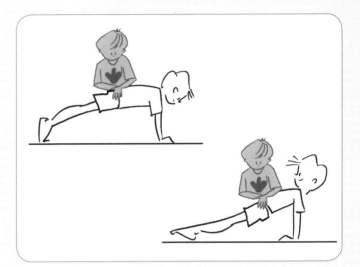

8. Shake and bake

- 1 partner in front support, other partner standing and holding his/her ankles.
- Standing partner gently shakes the legs up and down and side to side.
- Bottom partner resists any movement of the hips or trunk.
- Standing partner lets go of 1 foot, regrasps, then other foot, regrasps.
- Bottom partner resists having the legs come apart.

TECHNICAL PREPARATION FOR SPRING

try this ...

Whole group works on efficient 2-foot springs with Instructor. Various springs executed across the floor with efficient spring technique and arm swing.

1. SPRINGS across the floor

- 3 running steps then SPRING from 2 feet
- 3 running steps then SPRING twice from 2 feet
- 5 running steps SPRING, then 5 running steps spring, etc.

2. Bounding circuits

Use hoops and elevated surfaces (not higher than 1 box top)

- Emphasize good technical execution of each spring
- Emphasize good landing from the end of each sequence

3. Shapes in the air

- SPRING and make 'shapes' in air (tuck, straddle, dance-related shapes)
- Completely straighten body before landing
- Emphasize good SPRING technique, then good LANDING technique.

4. Beat board & mini-trampoline jumps

Beat board jumps, and mini-tramp jumps with good technique.

- Use a short run-up approach (5 running steps)
- Emphasize good technique, then good landing

5. One foot springs with instructor

Whole group works on efficient 1-foot SPRINGS with coach

- 1-foot spring for height (emphasize rigid body, and use arms efficiently)
- 1-foot SPRING onto elevated surfaces
- Series of dance leaps, (scissor leap, cat leap, tour jeté, and examples from RG)

COACH THE FOLLOWING: 2-arm SPRINGS

Groups of 4. Each participant coaches 1 of the following 2-arm spring activities.

1. Wheelbarrow walking

- Wheelbarrow walking (holding partner's knees, keeping trunk rigid).
- Have bottom gymnast lift up 1 leg at a time for partner to hold.
- Have top gymnast watch and listen to partner carefully to know when to stop.
- Top gymnast lowers 1 leg at a time.
- Bottom gymnast keeps body rigid all the time.

2. Monkey runs (front support with bent legs)

- Run legs and arms.
- Run legs, spring arms.
- Run arms, spring legs.
- Spring legs and arms.

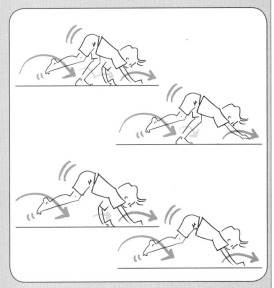

3. Windshield wiper

- Windshield wiper (hands on floor and feet elevated on box top).
- In front support, keep feet stationary and run with hands in 180° arc.
- Repeat back to starting position.
- Repeat several times (like windshield wipers on a car).
- Repeat springing from both hands instead of running.

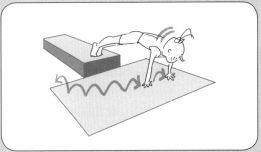

4. Sidewinder rattlesnake

- In front support, keep feet stationary, run with hands in 45° arc.
- Then keep hands stationary and run with the feet in 45° arc.
- Repeat several times as you progress across the floor.
- Repeat while springing from hands and then feet.

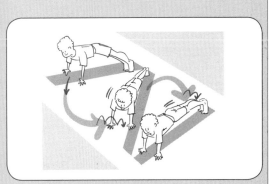

11
Locomotion

LOCOMOTION

LOCOMOTION is a movement pattern in which the body repetitively moves outside its base of support. The movement can be forward, backward, sideward or in any pattern. LOCOMOTION takes place in supports, in hangs, and on the feet. A key feature is the repetition of a basic motor activity. LOCOMOTOR activities can be performed individually or with a partner or group. They are suitable for all age groups and are building blocks for several gymnastics disciplines.

THE MECHANICS OF LOCOMOTION

Earlier we mechanically defined STATICS as any activity in which the body's centre of mass remains ...

Then we defined SPRING as a consequence of a force being rapidly applied to a body causing it to move out of its base of support.

Now we look at the situation where a body is repeatedly moved outside its base of support. We will call this type of movement LOCOMOTION. It includes walking, running and many other forms of locomotory activities.

Q | Complete   Q24

Where do we find locomotion?

Every gymnastics sport has some LOCOMOTION skills, and several sports have many.

However, in recreational and educational settings, there are innumerable examples of LOCOMOTIONS and many can be incorporated into games and circuits, which are excellent for developing physical and motor qualities as well as skill progressions.

For example, there are many animal walks and skipping activities that are ideal for positively stressing the cardiorespiratory system, which in turn, increases muscular endurance and cardiovascular endurance.

> **NOTE**
>
> Most gymnasts do not need a high degree of cardiorespiratory endurance for the actual competitive portion of their sport, but they all need high levels of muscular endurance in order to train effectively.

Lame monkey (leg raised)

Spring off both legs and walk the arms

Walk with legs, spring from both arms

Initiating locomotions

Most LOCOMOTIONS begin as STATIONARY POSITIONS such as supports and hangs. We will therefore study LOCOMOTIONS from front support, from back support, from cross support, and from hangs.

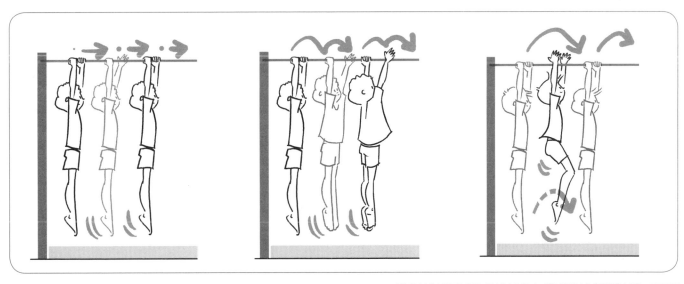

Animal Walks in Front Support

Monkey running (hands and feet)

Do the following moving forward, and then repeat moving backward:

- Run arms and legs.
- Run arms spring from legs.
- Spring from arms run legs.
- Spring from arms and legs.
- Lame monkey (1 leg raised).

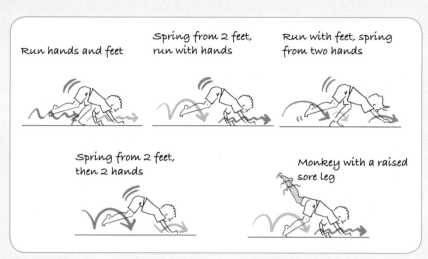

Run hands and feet   Spring from 2 feet, run with hands   Run with feet, spring from two hands

Spring from 2 feet, then 2 hands   Monkey with a raised sore leg

Inch worm

- Front support, walk feet forward to hands.
- Pike body as feet move toward hands.
- Repeat with hands now moving away from the feet back to front support.
- Repeat several times as you LOCOMOTE along the floor.

Sidewinder rattlesnake

- Front support, feet remain stationary .
- Run sideways on both arms so body rotates 90°, pivoting on feet.
- Then, hands remain stationary.
- Run sideways on both feet so body rotates 90°, pivoting on hands.
- Repeat several times as you locomote along the floor.

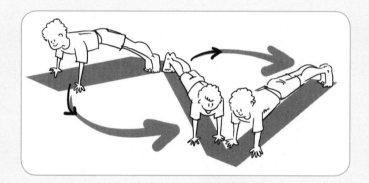

Mouse

- Front support with knees bent up to chest and arms bent, nose close to floor.
- Move forward by running on both feet and hands.
- Both arms and legs remain deeply bent throughout.

Water strider

- Front support, hips high.
- Spring upwards from both arms and legs.
- After several springs, spring across the floor.
- Spin in circles, left and then right, as you locomote across the floor.

Animal Walks in Back Support

Crab walk

- From back support with legs bent, arms straight
- Walk forward, then backward, then sideways left, then right
- Dizzy crab (erratic)
- Lame crab (1 limb raised off ground)

Cricket

- Similar to crab walk except both hands hop together, then both feet hop together
- Can be done forward or backward

Tarantula

- Arms and legs as wide as possible
- Similar to crab walk, except arms and legs are spread as wide as possible

Caterpillar

- 2, 3 or 4 gymnasts, all in crab walk, but joined together
- Joined by having gymnast in front place hands on feet of gymnast behind

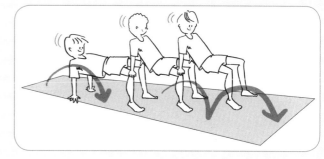

- Joined by having gymnast in front place hands on knees of gymnast behind

- Joined by having gymnast behind place feet on shoulders of gymnast in front

LOCOMOTION

Instructions

The class will be divided into large groups of 7-11. Each group will be assigned one of the LOCOMOTION activities below to present to others in the group.

After sufficient preparation, the coach will give a 2 minute presentation on the assigned task.

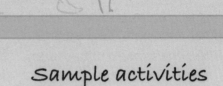

1. Walking (artistic and rhythmic gymnastics)
2. Skipping (aerobic, artistic and rhythmic gymnastics)
3. Chassés (aerobic, artistic and rhythmic gymnastics)
4. Dance steps (aerobic, artistic and rhythmic gymnastics)
5. Running (acrobatic, artistic and trampoline gymnastics)
   - Effective, powerful, without losing speed
   - Activities to develop good running motion
6. Locomotions (without spring) in front support
7. Locomotions (without spring) in back support
8. Locomotions (with spring) in front support
9. Other animal walks (elephants, birds, penguins, etc.)
10. Other locomotions (plane, train. etc.)

Sample activities

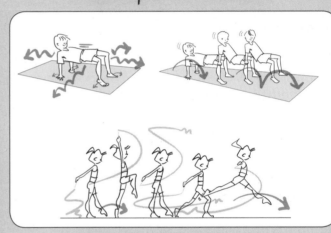

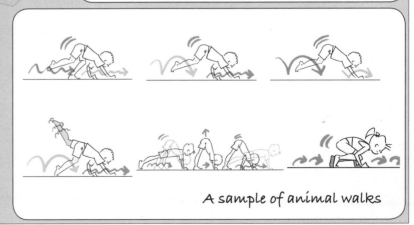

A sample of animal walks

12
Rotation

ROTATION

In all gymnastics sports, the majority of skills are from the ROTATION movement pattern.
The 3 axes that the body ROTATES about are:

1. The *longitudinal axis* with skills such as turns, pirouettes, pivots, spins, twists, etc.
2. The *transverse axis* with skills such as rolls, saltos, and bar circles
3. The *anterior / posterior axis* with skills such as sideward rolls, cartwheels

Label the axes in the diagram on the right.

MECHANICS OF ROTATION

Before we look at specific skills let's first understand that all ROTATIONS (regardless of the axis or sport) are generated or changed according to some simple mechanical principles, and almost all technical coaching of ROTATIONS is merely maximizing these simple mechanical principles or correcting errors in these mechanics.

ROTATIONS caused by off-centre forces

ROTATIONS are caused by off-centre forces (force not passing through the centre of mass).

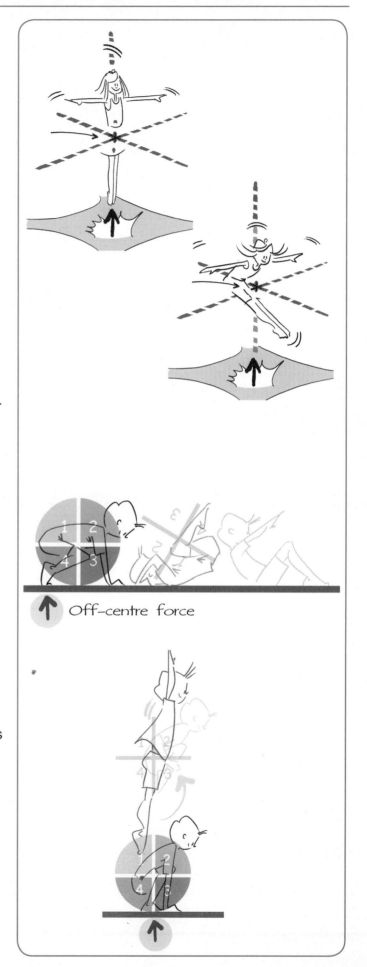

Off-centre force

Any force that is passing through the centre of mass will only generate linear motion (displacement).

Effect of Off-Centre Force

It should be clear that the further off-centre the force:

- The greater will be the ROTATION
- The less will be the displacement

Forces causing ROTATION

Study the adjacent example of a 2 foot take off and note the 2 off-centre forces each causing ROTATION

- Force #1 is from the leg push
- Force #2 is from the feet stopping after a fast run.

Example of a force couple

Study the adjacent example of 2 off-centre forces working together (as we do a jump full turn from our feet, or a hang on a bar and turn 180°).

Can you see that there are 2 forces (force couple)? Both are off-centre and both are rotating the body in the same direction.

 Complete Q25

1.

2.   180

180

NOTE to PARTICIPANTS

Pay particular attention to the following 8 activities as you will be coaching them at the end of the chapter.

Skills

1. Forward roll
2. Backward roll down a decline (wedge mat)
3. Cartwheel
4. Tour jeté
5. Spin full turn on one foot
6. Side shoulder roll
7. Jump full turn from mini trampoline
8. Skin the cat backward and forward on bars

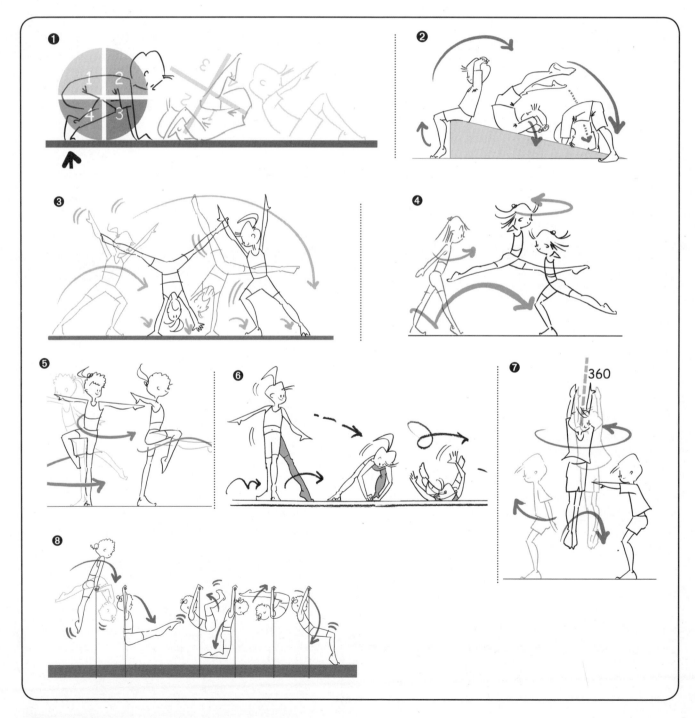

ROTATIONS ABOUT LONGITUDINAL AXIS

There are many examples of longitudinal axis ROTATIONS in all gymnastics sports. Practice these:

1. **Spins / turns on 1 foot and 2 feet**

   • Variety of turns and spins

2. **Jump turns from 2 foot SPRING**

   • From stand
   • From small elevation (below knee high)

3. **Jump turns from 1 foot SPRING**

   • Land on take-off foot
   • Land on other foot

4. **Front support to Back support to Front support**

   • Left and right

5. **Long hang, turn 360°**

   • Left and right

ROTATIONS ABOUT THE TRANSVERSE AXIS

FORWARD ROLL

Forward rolls are most easily taught using a decline (wedge mat or beat board with mats over).

The Roll Generator

The following is a method by which gymnasts can 'invent' hundreds of different forward rolls. Coaches can select rolls that will promote the development of ESP & F as well as the ABC'S.

Start in 1 position (squat) and finish your rolls in different finishing positions such as:

1. In straddle stand
2. On 1 foot
3. On 1 knee and 1 foot
4. ¼ turn to 2 knees
5. In V balance
6. Jump to forward landing on the hands
7. To tucked L balance
8. To bipod or tripod balance
9. To cross leg stand with ½ turn
10. To a shoulder balance

Reverse the Roll Generator

Now reverse the process and, finish in 1 position (squat), but start in different positions such as:

1. From a 1 leg stand
2. From kneeling
3. From 1 knee and 1 foot stand
4. From a front support
5. From a tripod balance
6. From a knee scale
7. From a straddle stand
8. From a headstand
9. From a cross leg stand with ½ turn

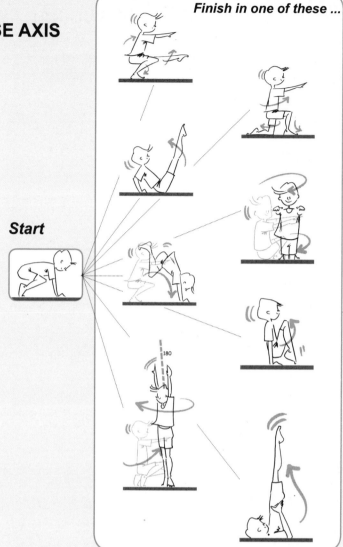

Finish in one of these ...

Start

Start in one of these ...

Finish

ROTATIONS ABOUT THE TRANSVERSE AXIS

BACKWARD ROLL

The backward roll is quite a difficult skill and should only be taught to those students who are flexible and strong enough to do all the progressions. It is possible, however, to help most participants to have a successful experience by teaching backward rolls down a decline (wedge mat).

Practise the following steps:

- Place your hands on top of your head, with your elbows spread wide (increase the base you are going to roll over)
- Squat and roll backward down the decline, rolling over your wide elbows
- Straddle your legs as you roll over your elbows and
- Place your feet (legs still straddled) quickly on the floor (same time as elbows are in contact)

NOTE
This sequence should allow for a successful learning experience, but doing a backward roll on a flat surface is considerably more difficult. It will be left for the next course where more progressions to develop flexibility and strength, will be given.

Follow-up activity

After success at the progression above for the backward roll, attempt the following modifications:

- Roll with legs together, bending knees only after the feet touch the mat
- Roll with palms facing upwards so you push off your hands
- Vary the finishing positions

Backward rolls are much easier if you have the inclination!

ROTATIONS ABOUT THE TRANSVERSE AXIS

The following activities are great for developing spatial orientation

TRANSVERSE ROTATIONS - APPARATUS

1. ***Roll forward from front hip support – low bars***

   - Finish in straight-arm hang
   - Finish in bent arm hang, legs tucked

2. ***Skin-the-cat on low bars***

   - Backward
   - Forward
   - Finish in L-hang

3. ***Combine #1 and #2***

   - Roll forward from front hip support to hang
   - Skin the cat backward, then forward

Pull over from stand to front hip support

4. ***Kick over from stack of mats or box***

   - 1 foot kick
   - 2 foot kick

5. ***Rotation sequence on low bar***

   - Forward roll on floor, finish under bar
   - Reach up behind to grasp bar
   - Forward skin-the-cat to stand
   - Jump to front hip support, roll forward, hang

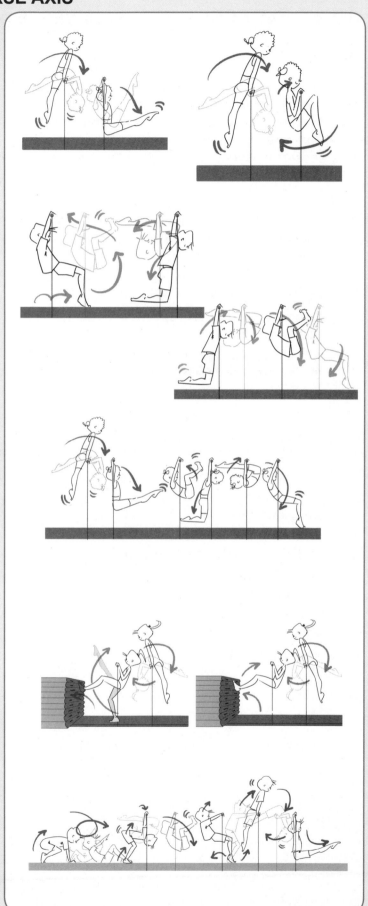

ROTATIONS ABOUT THE ANTERIOR – POSTERIOR AXIS

CARTWHEEL

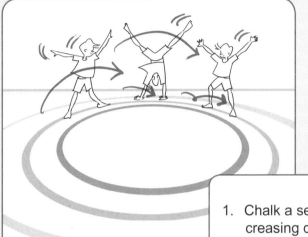

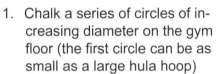

1. Chalk a series of circles of increasing diameter on the gym floor (the first circle can be as small as a large hula hoop)
2. Stand facing 'belly to the centre of the circle'
3. Place 1 hand then other hand, then 1 foot and the other foot sequentially on circle (left hand, right hand, right foot, left foot)
4. Once successful, move to larger circles until doing the cartwheel along a straight line

Cartwheel Generator

Like the forward roll example, we can 'invent' many cartwheels by changing the starting and finishing positions.

Vary the starting and finishing positions

1. Start on feet - finish on knees
2. Start on 1 knee and foot - finish on 1 foot
3. Start facing sideways
4. Start facing forwards

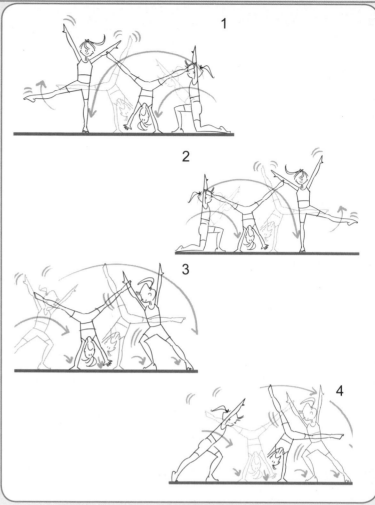

Vary arm positions and contact points

Cartwheels can be varied by changing the arm positions, and the contact points:

- Wide arms
- Narrow arms
- Crossed arms
- 1 arm
- Fists
- Elbows
- 1 hand, 1 fist

Arm postitions

More challenging

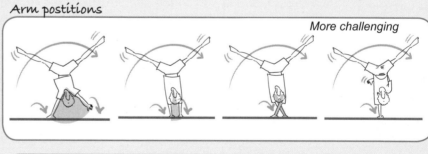

Contact points

PREPOSITIONAL ROTATIONS

On various elevated surfaces that are spread around the gym, take turns in pairs doing and coaching rotations (about all 3 axes) according to the instructor's 'prepositional instructions':

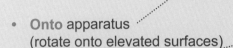

- **Onto** apparatus
  (rotate onto elevated surfaces)
- **On** apparatus
- **Off** apparatus
- **Over** apparatus
- **Around** apparatus

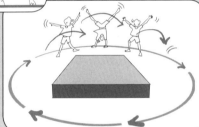

COACHING ROTATION

In Groups of 8, each participant will coach the following ROTATION skills to the rest of the group.

1. Forward roll
2. Backward roll down a decline (wedge mat)
3. Cartwheel
4. Tour jeté
5. Spin full turn on one foot
6. Side shoulder roll
7. Jump full turn from mini trampoline
8. Skin the cat forward and backward on bars

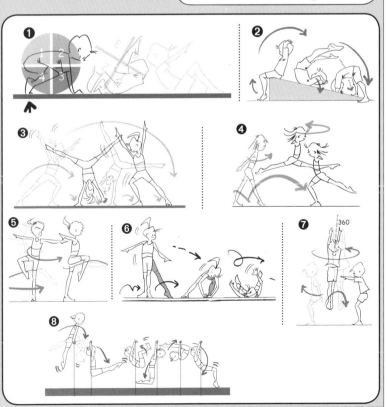

GYMNASTICS
FOUNDATIONS

Workbook

rotation

stationary positions

locomotion

spring

landings

GYMnastics
nastique
CANADA

National
Coaching
Certification
Program

Coaching
Association
of Canada

GYMNASTICS FOUNDATIONS questions

rotation

stationary positions

locomotion

spring

landings

Questions : Chapter 1
So You Want to Be a Coach

Q1   In groups of 2 or 3, list some brief descriptors of 'What is a coach?'

Q2   Discuss the following 5 questions with your partner(s), and make brief notes:

1. Is a coach a parent who coaches their child's community gymnastics program or their child's soccer team?

2. Is a coach someone who earns their living coaching a professional sports team?

3. Is a coach someone who has a Masters Degree in Kinesiology and teaches physical education, coaches high school teams, or volunteer coaches a team?

4. Is a coach a 16-year-old gymnast who coaches recreational classes?

5. Is coaching a profession? Is it a vocation? Is it a hobby?

Chapter 3 Fun

Q3

In groups of 3, each person suggests 1 way to make gymnastics more 'fun', and 1 way to make it less 'fun'. Record these in the space below and note any ideas from the class.

More Fun	Less Fun

Q4

In groups of 2 or 3, list characteristics of competitive sport training that are not desirable in a Community Sport initiation or developmental setting. Note additional ideas from the class.

Q5

In groups of 2 or 3, list some examples of ways to encourage BOTH playfulness AND fitness. Note any ideas from the class.

Chapter 4 Fitness

Q6   In groups of 2 or 3, discuss the term 'Strength' and jot down your definition. How close was your definition?

Q7   In groups of 2 or 3, discuss if a muscle always shortens when it contracts? Jot down your thoughts. Did you answer correctly?

Q8   In groups of 2 or 3, give 2 gymnastics examples of each mechanical state of muscle contraction. Correct your answers during the class discussion.

Q9   In groups of 2 or 3, name all the primary senses. Did you get them all?

Chapter 6 Fundamentals

Q10

In groups of 2 or 3, discuss the term Centre of Mass (Centre of Gravity). Can you describe what it is? Jot down your thoughts. How close was your description or definition?

Chapter 7 Stationary Positions

Q11

In groups of 2 or 3 (hopefully from different Sports), list 3 STATIONARY skills from different gymnastics sports. How did you do?

Sport 1 [   ]

Sport 2 [   ]

Sport 3 [   ]

Q12

Can you now group the STATIONARY skills you listed into some logical categories? Correct your answer during the class discussion.

Category 1 [   ]

Category 2 [   ]

Category 3 [   ]

Q13

In groups of 2 or 3, come up with several ways of making yourself more stable when you are in a STATIONARY position. How did you do?

1. _____

2. _____

3. _____

4. _____

5. _____

Chapter 8 Landings

Q14

In groups of 2 or 3, list examples of where LANDINGS occur in the different gymnastics sports. Can you give at least 1 example for each gymnastics sport? If not, add to your list during the class discussion.

AG: _____

AcG: _____

MAG: _____

RG: _____

WAG: _____

TG: _____

Q15

In groups of 2 or 3, describe one way to safely absorb the force of a LANDING. How did you do?

_____

_____

Q16

In groups of 2 or 3, discuss if there is a general (mechanical) principle we can apply to ALL safe LANDINGS? Jot down your answer. Were you right?

Q17

In groups of 2 or 3, jot down how you would decelerate when LANDING forward on your hands. Can you anticipate the technique and list the joints in the proper sequence as well? Were you right?

Q18

We have been discussing a general mechanical principle that is the basis for ALL SAFE LANDINGS. What is it?

Q19

Can you think of any other general mechanical principles that will help dissipate forces when LANDING with shoulder rolls?

Chapter 9 Teaching & Learning

Q20

In groups of 2 or 3, can you list 4 or 5 common time wasters and a solution for each? Record these in the space below and note any ideas from the class.

Time waster:

Solution:

Chapter 10 Spring

Q21

In groups of 2 or 3, discuss why rigid body exercises should be isometric and eccentric in nature. Jot down your ideas and share your answer with the class.

Q22

The muscles surrounding the trunk and hips are crucial for spring (rigid body). Can you identify them? How did you do?

Q23

In groups of 2 or 3, list 3 to 4 skills where this principle is used. Can you give at least 1 example for 3 different gymnastics sports? Complete your list during the class discussion.

AG:

AcG:

MAG:

RG:

WAG:

TG:

Chapter 11 Locomotion

Q24

In groups of 2 or 3 (hopefully from different Sports), list a minimum of 3 LOCOMOTION activities used in at least 2 different gymnastics sports. How did you do?

Sport 1 [   ]

Sport 2 [   ]

Sport 3 [   ]

Chapter 12 Rotation

Q25 In groups of 2 or 3, explain the mechanics of initiating the following skills.
Jot down your ideas and share your answers with the class.
How did you do?

Forward roll on mat:
_____
_____
_____

Cartwheel on mat:
_____
_____
_____

Jump turn to push-up position (AG)
_____
_____
_____

Rolling hoop along the floor (RG):
_____
_____
_____

Turntable 'front drop turn to front drop' (TG):
_____
_____

TABLE OF CONTENT

Introduction

Congratulations! You have completed the first phase of the training and certification program to become a coach in one of the 6 gymnastics sports. This workbook will help you develop your practical coaching skills as you work with a NCCP certified coach during a 10 week or longer recreational or precompetitive program.

The workbook is divided into 10 sections, each corresponding to one week in your coaching practicum. Each section includes:

- ✓ A review of certain concepts from the Gymnastics Foundations – Introduction course or from prior experience as an athlete or assistant coach
- ✓ New information to extend your knowledge base
- ✓ A planning and coaching task
- ✓ A reflection guide

The first three components will help you prepare to teach a portion of the lesson each week. Your supervisor must approve your task plan before the class. Once you have completed the first two tasks, you will teach your section of the lesson and assist your supervisor as required during the class. Afterwards you will complete a reflective activity with your supervisor. Your supervision is there to review your work and help you move forward for the next week's class.

Your Gymnastics Foundations Manual will serve as a valuable resource when you are completing your workbook activities. Your supervisor is also an important source of ideas and information. Observe and talk to other coaches in the gym. Use your imagination and be creative when you are developing games and activities. Most important, have FUN! If you show your gymnasts that you love gymnastics, they will also develop a love for our wonderful sport.

This workbook and your practical coaching experience must be completed before you register to attend the second weekend of training (Gymnastics Foundation Theory course, plus a Gymnastics Foundations Sport-Specific course).

Please bring your Gymnastics Foundations manual and completed workbook with you to the second course – you will need it to complete several tasks during the second course.

Note...

At no time should you be the only coach in charge of a group of participants.

You must always be working in tandem with a supervisor coach.
You will be able to assume responsibility for a group of gymnasts after the second weekend of training, when you achieve "Trained" coach status.

Before You Start...

Take a few minutes to record some basic information.

Your name:_____

Your address:_____

_____

Your phone number:_____

Your email:_____

Club name:_____

Club address:_____

_____

Club phone number:_____

Club email:_____

Club head coach's name:_____

Your supervisor's name:_____

Supervisor's phone number:_____

Supervisor's email:_____

Program name:_____

Program level:_____

Date of your Gymnastics Foundations Introduction course:_____

Location:_____

Learning facilitator's name:_____

Learning facilitator's phone number:_____

Learning facilitator's email:_____

P/T Gymnastics' phone number:_____

P/T Gymnastics' email:_____

P/T NCCP contact:_____

WEEK 1 - Review What You Know

How do the 3 components of GCG's Educational Philosophy guide your coaching?

*Fun:*_____

_____

*Fitness:*_____

_____

*Fundamentals:*_____

_____

_____

What are the three FUN principles?

_____

_____

_____

What are the eight PLAY guidelines?

_____

_____

_____

_____

_____

_____

_____

_____

List the 6 gymnastics sports. Circle the one(s) that you are coaching.

_____

_____

_____

WEEK 1 - Learn Something New

Finding out about your PROGRAM and your PARTICIPANTS

Prior to planning lessons for your participants, you need to obtain information about the logistics of your program. Complete the following tables - if you don't know the answers, ask your supervisor!

Location:_____

Group/Program name:_____Level:_____

Day:_____Time:_____

Number of participants:_____Gender:_____

Age range (youngest to oldest):_____

FACILITY - sketch the floor plan of the gym where your program takes place:

Do you share with other groups?_____If yes, how many?_____

Is there an established time-table for using equipment?_____

If yes, what is it?_____

What small equipment is available during your class time?_____

_____

_____

The second area of information that you will need is information about your participants. Complete the following Participant's Profile to gather information about one of your participants. Once again, if you don't know the answer to one of the questions, ask your supervisor. Eventually you should have this information about every person you coach.

Participant Profile Form

PHOTO

Name (first and last)_____

Nickname:_____

Phone number:_____

Email:_____

Date of birth (age):_____ Gender:_____

Height:_____ Weight:_____

Emergency contacts: Mother:_____

Father:_____

Guardian:_____

Drop-off/Pick-up person(s):   _____

Previous experience: _____

_____

Years in this program: _____Level:_____

Reasons for participating: _____

_____

Motivation (rewards):   _____

_____

Notes/comments (previous/chronic injuries, allergies, special needs, vacation dates, school, etc.):

_____

_____

_____

_____

_____

WEEK 1 – Shadow Coach

Being professional

- Before you go to the gym, make sure you are properly dressed for coaching (club t-shirt or other required uniform, no jewellery, hair tied back, etc.).

- Arrive at the gym at least 15 minutes before the start of your class so you can speak with your supervisor and receive last minute instructions.

- Assist with equipment set-up and tear-down.

- When the participants arrive for their class, smile and introduce yourself.

- Use this 1st class to get to know as much as you can about the program and the participants:

  - ❑ Get a copy of the class list. Start to learn the participant's names. Become aware of each participant's behaviour patterns (level of cooperation, things they like/fear, etc.)

  - ❑ Get a copy of the lesson plan and note the kinds of activities planned for each part of the lesson.

  - ❑ Work alongside your supervisor coach. Listen and watch. Save your questions for after the lesson.

  - ❑ Become familiar with established routines for taking attendance, warm-up, cool-down, moving between equipment stations, etc.

WEEK 1 - Reflection

Questions for your supervisor coach?

Use the space below to write your questions before your meeting with your supervisor and add your supervisor's answers.

WEEK 2 – Review What You Know

Beginnings & Endings

Meeting & Greeting: What activities does a coach include at the beginning of the class?

Why is a proper *warm-up* valuable?

How do the *3 F's* relate to warm-up?

What is the purpose of the *cool-down*?

Closing & Goodbye: What activities does a coach include in the ending of the class?

WEEK 2 – Learn Something New

Learning styles

Have you ever considered how you learn the best? Do you have to see a move in order to learn it, or is a verbal explanation all you need? Do you get nowhere until you try the move itself? Has a specific word or phrase given you a mental picture that has made all the difference in your learning? Learning experts have identified three Learning Styles:

Visual learners receive information by watching a demonstration, a video, or looking at a sketch, photo or diagram. Pointing out specific things to watch for in a demonstration helps them when learning skills. Colour coding can also be useful.

Auditory learners receive information through their ears. Explanations, counting or clapping rhythms, hearing cues or counts, helps them learn skills. Auditory learners who are exposed simply to a visual presentation will try to make up their own verbal cues in their heads to supply the missing 'voice'.

Kinesthetic learners try moves and learn from the feedback their own muscles, joints and skin gives them. Tactile cues, like "*feel your shoulder muscles touching your ears in a handstand*" or "*feel your big toe knuckles touching each other*" draw their attention to the kinesthetic feedback that helps them learn. At times a coach may need to place or position them, or move their limbs through a movement so that they can feel it correctly.

What is your preferred learning style?

The following questionnaire is designed to help you discover your preferred learning style. To a large extent, your preferred learning style is linked to the sensory channel (hearing, seeing, feeling) you use the most to learn. In the 20 situations described, circle the option (A, B, or C) that best describes your personal experience.

What happens when...

1. **You're planning a series of technique progressions for the next lesson:**
   A. You make lots of gestures with your hands while you think.
   B. You draw up a diagram to help you clarify a few key ideas.
   C. You mentally go over the key points and cues that you are going to say.

2. **You're getting ready to write up work for the course you're taking:**
   A. You are taken aback by the pile of paper.
   B. You feel tired even before you begin.
   C. You scold yourself for waiting until now to get to the work.

3. **You're off to the gym:**
   A. You are delighted to see that the sky is clear.
   B. You hear birds singing and it is really delightful.
   C. You yawn and wish you could stay in bed.

4. **You go into the coaches' lounge and the first thing you notice is:**
   A. The sounds of conversations.
   B. A new gymnastics poster on the wall.
   C. The smell of coffee.

5. **You go to gather some other coaches to attend a staff meeting:**
   A. You hear them chatting, unaware the meeting is about to start.
   B. You hurry them along so that they get into the room as quickly as possible.
   C. You see that they are not ready to go into the meeting

6. **You walk into the gym to begin teaching your class:**
   A. You hope the heating will be switched on soon; it's cold in the room.
   B. You notice the last group left the area untidy.
   C. You're upset by the gymnasts who continue chatting.

7. **Your group is waiting for you to start the lesson. As you walk over:**
   A. You wonder what they are whispering about.
   B. You notice that two 'challenging' participants are sitting next to each other.
   C. You're not sure where to be: sitting down or standing up.

8. **An athlete comes to see you to ask you a question:**
   A. The fact that he/she is looking anxious is not a surprise.
   B. You wonder what's behind his/her approach.
   C. You're amused that he/she is coming to see you.

9. **You're writing your gymnasts' report card and feedback forms:**
   A. Your hand will go to sleep if you go on any longer.
   B. You try to figure if your handwriting is legible.
   C. The music on your iPod makes the time go by faster.

10. **Your athletes don't understand an explanation:**
    A. You immediately think about how to explain it another way.
    B. You're surprised at the number of puzzled faces in front of you.
    C. You immediately demonstrate the skill again.

11. **Two athletes challenge the coach, and you notice:**
    A. That it makes everyone uncomfortable.
    B. That they speak without asking permission.
    C. That they look very angry.

12. **Some athletes ask to discuss a problem that everyone in the club is talking about:**
    A. You think their request is out of line.
    B. You're touched by their request.
    C. You note that the other people present agree with the request.

13. **The gymnasts are surprised when you announce the next special activity:**
    A. Even though it's been posted on the schedule for a long time.
    B. Even though they know what to do anyway.
    C. Even though you'd repeated it several times.

14. **You're taking your group to do a mall demonstration:**
    A. You notice your new shoes are very comfortable.
    B. You're delighted to see the smiling faces of the people who are watching.
    C. You check the numbers several times to be sure everyone's there.

15. **You're summoned to your head coach's office:**
    A. You've made up your mind to stand firm on this issue.
    B. You wonder whether this is a good omen or not.
    C. You re-read the memo to see if you can find an explanation.

16. **A meeting is just about to start:**
    A. You notice person X isn't there.
    B. You work out how long the meeting will last by figuring on ten minutes per agenda item.
    C. You notice you've chosen a more comfortable seat than last time.

17. You approach the parents of some athletes with whom you've arranged a meeting:
A. You notice they have a slight regional accent.
B. You extend your hand to them spontaneously.
C. Just a moment! You thought they were older than this.

18. A supervisor walks into your work area:
A. You find he/she has a pleasant voice.
B. You notice a band-aid on his/her hand.
C. You have a dry throat.

19. In the cafeteria, you're swallowing the last few mouthfuls of your meal:
A. You've enjoyed the meal.
B. The conversation around you isn't loud: so much the better!
C. You find the colour of the dishes brighter than usual.

20. Once the day is over, you go home and you:
A. Congratulate yourself for the successful moments of the day.
B. Re-live the good moments of the day.
C. Enjoy sitting down after a day on your feet.

Scoring the questionnaire:

The table below shows what kind of learning each answer in the questionnaire represents. For example, choosing the answer B for the first question indicates a visual learning style. For each situation in the questionnaire, circle the letter that corresponds to your answer for the situation. Now find the total for each of the three columns in the table. To do this, assign A answers the value 1, B answers the value 2, and C answers the value 3, and add the values for each column. The column with the highest total represents your primary learning style.

Situation	Visual	Auditory	Kinesthetic
1	B	C	A
2	A	C	B
3	A	B	C
4	B	A	C
5	C	A	B
6	B	C	A
7	B	A	C
8	A	B	C
9	B	C	A
10	B	A	C
11	C	B	A
12	C	A	B
13	A	C	B
14	B	C	A
15	C	B	A
16	A	B	C
17	C	A	B
18	B	A	C
19	C	B	A
20	B	A	C
Total			

How does the existence of different learning styles (visual, auditory, and kinesthetic) affect how you coach? What concrete steps can you take to give each participant the opportunity to learn in his or her preferred way?

Visual Learners...

General observations

- 👍 Often do better when shown rather than told. May have difficulty understanding oral directions.
- 👍 Have a tendency to watch your face when they are read or spoken to.
- 👍 Like to look at books and pictures.
- 👍 Like things orderly and neat. Often dress in an attractive manner.
- 👍 Can generally find things that are lost and seldom misplace their own things.
- 👍 Can often recall where they saw something some time ago.
- 👍 Notice details. Are good proofreaders, see typing errors, & notice if your clothing has a flaw.
- 👍 Can find pages or places in a book quite easily.
- 👍 Often draw reasonably well — at least with good balance and symmetry.
- 👍 May use few words when responding to questions; they may rarely talk in class.

Recommended teaching methods

- ☑ Give visual directions and demonstrations as often as possible.
- ☑ Point out specific things to look for during a demonstration.
- ☑ Use visual aids such as drawings, videos, photographs, overheads, etc.
- ☑ Use colour-coding systems and visual aids.

Auditory Learners...

General observations

- 👍 Follow oral instructions easily.
- 👍 Remember spoken words or ideas quite well. May answer better when questions are explained to them verbally compared to when they must read them.
- 👍 Like musical and rhythmic activities.
- 👍 Tend to memorize easily, and often know all the words to songs.
- 👍 Will memorize a dance or floor exercise routine by linking movement to the music.
- 👍 Are often referred to as talkers and are seldom quiet. Tell jokes and tall tales and are full of excuses for why something isn't done.
- 👍 May appear physically awkward.
- 👍 Often have a poor perception of space and may get lost in unfamiliar surroundings.
- 👍 Often have poor perception of time and space and often do not keep track of time easily.
- 👍 Often have mixed laterality (left hand – right footed).

Recommended teaching methods

- ☑ Teach them to talk through the steps in a task or activity.
- ☑ Provide verbal cues and/or counts.
- ☑ Encourage them to think out loud, and listen to what they are saying.
- ☑ Use tape-recorded instructions.
- ☑ Use lots of audio equipment in the learning process.
- ☑ Pair the individual with a visual learner.

Kinesthetic Learners...

General observations

- 👍 Learn best by doing and exploring the environment.
- 👍 Move around a lot and are sometimes considered hyperactive.
- 👍 Seem to want to feel and touch everything.
- 👍 Are usually quite well co-ordinated.
- 👍 Enjoy working with their hands. Like to take things apart and to put things together.
- 👍 May truly enjoy writing things down.

Recommended teaching methods

- ☑ Use movement exploration.
- ☑ Have them tap tempos.
- ☑ Point out how a movement feels. They will be very aware of muscle tension and relaxation. They may have well-developed spatial awareness.
- ☑ For low-risk movements, demonstrate the whole skill; then let them try it.
- ☑ Use concrete objects as learning aids, especially ones that can be manipulated easily. For instance, have them place a piece of foam between their ankles when learning to keep their legs together.

Learning experts also recognise the role that the imagination plays in learning, although they have not identified the imagination pathway as a style. Images are vivid descriptive comparisons that create a mental picture. Examples include:

- ☑ *"Sit like you've just got in the bathtub & the water's freezing"* (off-tramp seat drop training)
- ☑ *"Find a place on the mat that is large enough for you to make a snow angel without touching anyone"* (teaching concept of personal space)
- ☑ *"Motorcycle position"* (teaching landing position)

Write your own examples here:

1. _____
_____
2. _____
_____
3. _____
_____
4. _____
_____
5. _____
_____

If we are aware that the people we coach have a variety of learning styles, we can plan our teaching in ways that will help all our participants to learn. We can make sure all our participants can **watch, listen & try** in equal amounts. And, we can use our imagination to find images that will appeal to their imagination.

WEEK 2 - Create and Plan

In preparation for this week's lesson, you will be leading an active game to begin the warm-up and a quiet activity for the cool-down. Describe these activities below:

WARM-UP game/activity:_____

Equipment needed:_____

_____

_____

Rules of play:_____

_____

_____

Set-up formation:

Why did you choose this game/activity?_____

_____

_____

What SAFETY considerations should you keep in mind? How will you manage them?_____

_____

_____

_____

_____

Which of the PLAY GUIDELINES will you follow to ensure the game is fun for all participants?

_____

_____

_____

How will you explain or demonstrate this game to accommodate all LEARNING STYLES?

_____

_____

_____

_____

COOL-DOWN game/activity:_____

Equipment needed:_____

_____

_____

Rules of play:_____

_____

_____

Set-up formation:

Why did you choose this game/activity?_____

_____

_____

What SAFETY considerations should you keep in mind? How will you manage them?_____

_____

_____

_____

_____

Which of the PLAY GUIDELINES will you follow to ensure the game is fun for all participants?

_____

_____

_____

How will you explain or demonstrate this game to accommodate all LEARNING STYLES?

_____

_____

_____

_____

WEEK 2 – Coach

Coaching Tasks:

❑ Discuss your warm-up and cool-down activities with your supervisor coach.
❑ Discuss how you will assist your coach during the rest of the lesson.
❑ Lead your games.
❑ Assist where required.
❑ Observe the participants and try to discover their learning styles. Complete chart below.

Name of Participant	Preferred learning style?	How can I help this person learn?

WEEK 2 - Reflection

WARM-UP game/activity:_____

What worked well?_____
_____
_____

How did the participants react to my instructions?_
_____
_____

Did anything not work well? Why?_____
_____
_____

What would I change for next time?_____
_____
_____

Supervisor comments and other notes:_____
_____
_____

COOL-DOWN game/activity:_____

What worked well?_____
_____
_____

How did participants react to my instructions?___
_____
_____

Did anything not work well? Why?_____
_____
_____

What would I change for next time?_____
_____
_____

Supervisor comments and other notes:_____
_____
_____

WEEK 3 - Review What You Know

What are the 5 Fundamental Movement Patterns (FMPs) common to all gym sports?

1. _____ 4. _____
2. _____ 5. _____
3. _____

What is the value of grouping gymnastics skills into just 5 FMPs?

_____
_____
_____

Why are stationary positions so important in gymnastics?

_____
_____
_____

What are the 3 TYPES of stationary positions? Distinguish between them briefly.

1. _____
2. _____
3. _____

Give 6 EXAMPLES of stationary positions that must be mastered in your gym sport.

1. _____ 4. _____
2. _____ 5. _____
3. _____ 6. _____

What is the definition of Centre of mass?

_____
_____
_____

What is the definition of Base of support?

_____
_____

WEEK 3 – Learn Something New

Safety in the Gym

Imagine that a parent comes up to you in the gym and says, "What are the risks in your program? What steps are you taking to keep my child safe? How will you respond to this parent? Use the table below to answer these questions.

Risks of my Sport	My actions to make classes as safe as possible

Does your club have any safety rules posted? Copy them down here.

Are there any areas in the facility that concern you re safety?

WEEK 3 - Create and Plan

This week your task is to create or select & plan 3 activities to develop your gymnasts' ability to hold a stationary position. Ask your supervisor where these activities will fit in the lesson: as part of the warm-up, as part of 1 or more of the teaching activities or as part of the cool-down. Select activities that are fun, safe & age appropriate. Remember to use teaching methods that will reach visual, auditory and kinesthetic learners.

Suggestions:
1. An immunity tag game where the safe position is a stationary position.
2. A group of paired cooperative activities requiring balance.
3. A group of fitness activities to develop core strength in held positions.

Activity 1:

Activity 2:

Activity 3:

WEEK 3 – Coach

Coaching Tasks

❑ Discuss your activities with your supervisor coach before the lesson.

❑ Discuss how you will assist your coach during the rest of the lesson.

❑ Lead your activities – review each stationary position by naming and demonstrating it – have the gymnasts practice the stationary position – observe, give feedback & help if necessary.

❑ Assist where required.

WEEK 3 – Reflection

Activity 1_____	Activity 2_____	Activity 3_____
What worked well?_____	What worked well?_____	What worked well?_____
How did class respond to instructions?	How did class respond to instructions?	How did class respond to instructions?
Did anything not work well? Why?_____	Did anything not work well? Why?_____	Did anything not work well? Why?____
What would you change for next time?	What would you change for next time?	What would you change for next time?
Discuss your self-assessment with your supervisor & note additional things that you need to remember or work on:	Discuss your self-assessment with your supervisor & note additional things that you need to remember or work on:	Discuss your self-assessment with your supervisor & note additional things that you need to remember or work on:?

WEEK 4 - Review What You Know

Landings

Why it is it so important to master correct landing technique?

> 1. _____
> 2. _____

What were the 3 types of landings covered during the Gymnastics Foundations course?

> 1. _____
> 2. _____
> 3. _____

What is the key biomechanical principle for landings on the feet?

> _____
> _____

What is the key biomechanical principle for landings with too much rotation?

> _____
> _____

WEEK 4 - Learn Something New

Keys to Successful Coaching

What is the secret to being a successful coach? It may be summarized in 3 words, known as the 3 Ps:

> **Personality - Preparation - Presentation**

Personality

If a coach's personality is enthusiastic, understanding and patient, then the most important prerequisite for successful coaching has been satisfied. It is important that you be able to:

- 👍 Captivate and motivate your class.
- 👍 Help your gymnasts overcome their fears and inhibitions.
- 👍 Energize your participants to reach beyond their own known ability.

How can you improve your teaching personality?

👍 Picture yourself "sparkling" in front of the class

👍 Observe and emulate coaches who have that enthusiasm and confidence

👍 Ask for feedback from your supervisors or peers

Preparation

The best lessons are those that have been thoroughly prepared. Visualizing how you want the lesson to run ideally and having alternate back-up plans in case adjustments have to be made is the key to successful lessons.

Presentation

Teaching Styles

There is a continuum of teaching styles that has at one end, teacher-led styles and at the other end, learner-led styles. An example of the former is the drill or progression style and an example at the latter is the discovery or problem-solving style. Make no mistake about the fact that the teacher is always in charge! A competent coach can function in both styles and provides novelty and interest to the gymnasts by smoothly switching back and forth between the styles depending on the nature of the task and the readiness of the gymnasts.

Teacher-led

When it is important that a skill be performed in a specific way (often the safest way), the coach uses a DIRECT style. The coach:

✓ Names the skill and explains its purpose

✓ Demonstrates the skill or has it shown

✓ Presents a series of progressions

✓ Gives frequent feedback to the group & to individuals

✓ Rewards gymnasts who approach correct execution of the skill

---

Learner-led

When the basic skill is less risky, when the coach is confident that the participants can achieve it safely, and when specific correct technique is not important, the coach uses a DISCOVERY or PROBLEM-SOLVING style. The coach:

✓ Sets a challenge

✓ Asks a question: "*How many ways can you…?*"

✓ Encourages creativity

✓ Accepts a wide variety of responses

Planning how participants will practice

The coach also has options for setting up the way the participants will learn skills:

👍 *Learning en masse* where everyone has a space to practice independently.

👍 *Stations* where equipment is set out so that there is 1 station per participant (or pair). The gymnasts stay at each station for a pre-determined length of time.

👍 Learning through *well-designed games* that develop skills and fitness.

👍 *Circuits* where equipment is set out in a circle or weave formation that allows participants to move from 1 piece to the next.

WEEK 4 - Create and Plan

This week you will design a series of activities to enable participants to practise a variety of landings. Assume that these landings have been taught in previous lessons. Discuss with your supervisor coach which area and what equipment will be available for these activities. You will need to 'design' 8 different landing activities. Sketch the activities in the table below. **Make a sign for each activity and post it for your visual learners.**

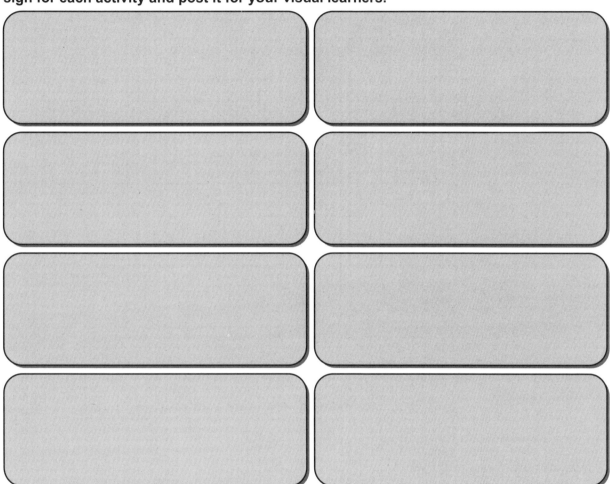

WEEK 4 - Coach

Coaching Tasks

❑ Discuss your landing activities/stations with your supervisor coach.

❑ Discuss how you will assist your coach during the rest of the lesson.

❑ Post your signs.

❑ Lead your activities – review each landing by naming & demonstrating it – have the gymnasts practice the landing – observe, give feedback and help if necessary.

❑ Assist where required.

WEEK 4 - Reflection

What worked well?_____

_____

_____

How did the participants respond to your instructions? To the illustrations?_____

_____

_____

Did anything not go as planned? Why? How would you fix this problem?_____

_____

_____

What would you change the next time you lead these activities?_____

_____

_____

Assess yourself on the three 'Ps' during this lesson: circle the score that you think you rate on a scale of 1 to 10, where 10 is excellent!

Personality	1	2	3	4	5	6	7	8	9	10
Preparation	1	2	3	4	5	6	7	8	9	10
Presentation	1	2	3	4	5	6	7	8	9	10

Discuss your reflections and self-assessment with your supervisor coach & note additional things that you need to remember:

_____

_____

_____

_____

_____

_____

_____

_____

_____

_____

_____

WEEK 5 – Review What You Know

Locomotion and Spring

Define locomotion.

_____

_____

Describe efficient running technique.

_____

_____

Explain how the principles of spring are the reverse of the principles of landing.

_____

_____

Name 3 skills requiring spring in your sport.

1. _____
2. _____
3. _____

Gives 6 examples for each of the following:

Locomotions – ANIMAL WALKS
1. _____ 4. _____
2. _____ 5. _____
3. _____ 6. _____

Locomotions – NON-ANIMAL WALKS (e.g. walking forward)
1. _____ 4. _____
2. _____ 5. _____
3. _____ 6. _____

Springs – ANIMAL WALKS
1. _____ 4. _____
2. _____ 5. _____
3. _____ 6. _____

Springs – NON-ANIMAL WALKS (e.g. walking forward)
1. _____ 4. _____
2. _____ 5. _____
3. _____ 6. _____

WEEK 5 – Learn Something New

Using Circuits

Your Gymnastics Foundations Manual has many suggestions for using circuits. A circuit may or may not use equipment, but it always includes a variety of activities or exercises that allow a group of gymnasts to be continuously active while they develop skills and/or fitness. Besides being used to reinforce learning and to develop fitness, circuits are also a great way to add variety to your program and to challenge your participants.

Guidelines

👍 A circuit must have enough activities to keep all the participants in the group active. As a rule, there should be at least 1 more activity than there are participants.

👍 The activities should require no spotting and must be safe.

👍 The pathways between activities must be clearly designated to prevent collisions.

👍 Explanations must be simple, clear and quick so that the gymnasts can start quickly.

👍 Start the gymnasts at different activities in the circuit to avoid long line-ups.

👍 Suggest that if a line-up occurs, they skip that activity and go to the next activity.

👍 Activities should be easy to change to vary the circuit and make it more challenging, or to offer easier options for those having difficulty, to add novelty, etc.

WEEK 5 – Create and Plan

Your task this week is to design a circuit for practising either locomotion or spring. Of course, landing on the feet and hands will be required as well! Use the space below, to design a locomotion or spring circuit for a group of 6 to 8 participants who are just starting out in your sport.

Age of participants:_____   Locomotion ☐   Spring ☐

Now imagine that you have a group of older gymnasts who have been doing gymnastics for 3 years. How would you change the activities to accommodate this older group? Or imagine that you have a group of 3 to 5 year old gymnasts who have just started gymnastics. How would you change the activities to accommodate this younger group? Pick an age group and adjust your circuit.

*Age of participants:*_____   *Locomotion* ☐   *Spring* ☐

Discuss your circuits with your supervisor. Make the necessary adjustments to implement one of your circuits with your group.

Don't forget the following points when planning your circuit:

*How and when will you set up the circuit?*_____
_____

*How will you explain / demonstrate the activities?*_____
_____
_____

*How much time will you allocate to this circuit?*_____

*How will you supervise the circuit? Where will you stand?*_____
_____
_____

*What corrections will you make? How will you give feedback?*_____
_____
_____

*Will you use music? If yes, how will you coordinate it with the circuit?*_____
_____

WEEK 5 - Coach

Coaching Tasks

☐ Discuss your circuit with your supervisor coach.
☐ Discuss how you will assist your coach during the rest of the lesson.
☐ Set up and lead your circuit – introduce each activity – have the gymnasts run through the circuit – observe, give feedback and change is necessary.
☐ Assist where required.

WEEK 5 - Reflection

*What worked well?*_____

_____

*How did the participants respond to your instructions? To your corrections?*_____

_____

_____

*Did anything not go as planned? Why? How would you fix this problem?*_____

_____

_____

*What would you change the next time you lead this circuit?*_____

_____

_____

What are your impressions of the progress of the participants under your care?
 Are they having fun?   Yes   No
 Do they appear to be improving their strength and flexibility?   Yes   No
 Are they learning skills?   Yes   No

You are almost half-way through your practical coaching experience. What is the most important thing that you have learned to date? How has it helped you?

_____

_____

Discuss your reflections and self-assessment with your supervisor coach & note additional things that you need to remember:

_____

_____

_____

WEEK 6 - Review What You Know

Physical Abilities (ESP)

Complete the table to show that you understand the difference between endurance, strength and power. Use your Gymnastics Foundations manual to complete the table.

	Endurance	Strength	Power
Definition			
2 skills my gymnasts do that require this physical attribute			
3 ways to develop it in a fun way			

WEEK 6 - Learn Something New

What is Self-esteem?

Self-esteem is the way a person sees himself or herself. Self-esteem can be affected by comments, positive or negative, from others, including messages about the person's participation in sport.

The Importance of Self-esteem

One of the most important stages in the development of self-esteem occurs between the ages of 6 and 11. As a coach, you have an important role to play in the development of self-esteem in your gymnasts.

Seemingly harmless comments may have a significant impact. Try to find something that the gymnast does well, even when you are making corrections. Positive comments may focus on the way the gymnast performs a particular skill or on aspects not directly linked to performance, for example, respecting the rules, being on time, taking care of the equipment, making others laugh, or helping others.

As a coach, what you say (verbally or through your body language) is extremely important in the eyes of the athletes, and you may have direct influence on their self-esteem. You must always assess the potential impact of the words you say to your gymnasts or the comments you make to them.

Here are some indications that a participant may be lacking self esteem:

☹ Avoids doing a task or responding to a challenge or gives up at the first opportunity.

☹ Shows signs of regression and acts like a baby or in an immature way for their age.

☹ Behaves extremely stubbornly to hide feelings of incompetence, frustration, or helplessness.

☹ Makes excuses ("*the coach is stupid*") or makes light of events ("*this is a dumb sport anyway*").

☹ Has mood swings, appears sad, weeps, has fits of anger or frustration, or has periods of silence.

☹ Makes negative comments about himself or herself such as "*I never do anything well*", "*Nobody likes me*", "*I'm not pretty*", "*It's my fault…*"

☹ Sensitive to praise and criticism.

☹ Excessively worried about the opinion of others.

☹ Significantly affected by the negative influence of friends.

Remember that part of your coaching role is to help all participants develop self-esteem. It is important that you set a positive, respectful tone in the gym at all times and will all the participants. Be aware of how the gymnasts interact. Praise them for supporting each other; do not tolerate teasing or bullying.

Below are some suggestions for setting the tone:

👍 Greet all participants warmly when they arrive, and make sure they are happy to be there.

👍 Show them you are confident in their ability to learn.

👍 Show them respect.

👍 Tell them what they do well.

👍 Show them you appreciate them as people.

👍 Communicate with them in a positive manner.

👍 Engage them in activities appropriate for their level of development. Have realistic objectives and expectations based on their level.

👍 Provide sincere and frequent praise, e.g. encourage them three or four times before making corrections. Encourage gymnasts to try without always putting the emphasis on results.

👍 Avoid elimination games, having peers select team members and games that put pressure on participants. Create situations in which participants have a good chance of being successful.

👍 Be precise when you praise their efforts or performance.

👍 Congratulate them on their special achievements; recognize each gymnast's progress.

👍 Smile, wink, or nod to athletes to acknowledge their efforts. A pat on the back is a great way to encourage athletes.

👍 Give athletes responsibility. Have them participate in decision making and give everyone the opportunity to be the leader. Alternate the role of captain.

👍 Seek the opinion of athletes, and encourage them to ask questions.

👍 Communicate the true joy of doing gymnastics.

Building self-esteem in your participants

Think about your interactions with your gymnasts. Identify the ways you have been affecting their self-esteem. Be honest! Now fill in your action plan:

I will STOP... _____
_____
_____

*I will CONTINUE...*_____
_____
_____

I will START... _____
_____
_____

WEEK 6 – Create and Plan

This week your task is to create or select and plan 3 activities for developing leg and/or arm strength or endurance. Ask your supervisor where these activities will fit in the lesson (as part of the warm-up, as part of 1 or more of the teaching activities or as part of the cool-down). Select activities that are fun, safe and age appropriate. Remember to use teaching methods that will reach visual, auditory and kinesthetic learners. Refer to your Gymnastics Foundations Manual for ideas.

Activity 1:

Activity 2:

Activity 3:

WEEK 6 - Coach

Coaching Tasks

- ❑ Discuss your activities with your supervisor coach.
- ❑ Discuss how you will assist your coach during the rest of the lesson.
- ❑ Lead your activities – explain and demonstrate – have the gymnasts practice the activities – observe, give feedback and help as necessary.
- ❑ Assist where required.

WEEK 6 - Reflection

What are your impressions of the self-esteem of the participants under your care?

Does everyone show signs of having a good self-esteem?	Yes	No
Does everyone seem 'comfortable' or at ease in the gym?	Yes	No
Did you try to implement your self-esteem building action?	Yes	No
Did you discuss ways to improve self-esteem with your supervisor?	Yes	No

*What worked well?*_____
_____
_____

How did the participants respond to your instructions? _____
_____
_____

*Did anything not go as planned? Why? How would you fix this problem?*_____
_____
_____

*What would you change the next time you do these activities?*_____
_____
_____
_____

Discuss your reflections with your supervisor coach & note additional things that you need to remember:
_____
_____
_____
_____

WEEK 7 – Review What You Know

Flexibility

What do we mean when we say that a gymnast is flexible?

Name 3 skills that require flexibility in your gymnastic sport.

List some of the reasons why flexibility is important.

What is the difference between the active and the passive range of movement?

Static flexibility activities are best done at the end of the practice because the muscles are adequately warmed up at that time, intense effort is not required, and the pace of the exercises encourages relaxation and cooling down. In fact, research has shown that slow static stretching in the warm-up reduces explosive power in the muscles and is detrimental to performance in activities requiring powerful take-offs (leaps and jumps, tumbling, vaulting). While gymnasts are stretching, the coach can conclude the lesson (make announcements, give out papers, etc.)

With recreational participants, flexibility exercises are generally performed without the help of a partner. The muscle group is stretched in a controlled and gradual manner, without any interruption of the movement, until a slight tension is felt. Then that position is held from 10 to 20 seconds, depending on the age and motivation of the participant. It is important to breathe slowly & deeply. Repeat each stretch 2 to 3 times, depending on time available. Stretch on both sides.

Describe 3 'exercises' that make slow static stretching fun for recreational gymnasts.

WEEK 7 – Learn Something New

Emergency Action Plan

Do you know what to do if you are confronted with an emergency while coaching? Locate a copy of your gym club's Emergency Action Plan (EAP) information sheet and read it thoroughly. Keep a copy of your club's EAP with your workbook.

Describe what you would do if confronted with the following situation in your gym? List each step in order. Refer to your club's EAP and ask your supervisor to verify your answer.

Two of your gymnasts collided and bumped heads while playing a vigorous game. One seems dazed and unsteady. Within a minute she drops to the floor. The other has a gash above the eye. What do you do?

_____
_____
_____
_____
_____
_____
_____
_____
_____
_____

WEEK 7 – Create and Plan

Design a warm-up that includes a cardio activity and a fun activity that develops flexibility for your group of participants.

Activity 1 (Cardio):

Activity 2 (Flexibility):

Design a cool down focussing on developing flexibility for your group of participants.

Cool-down (flexibility):

Remember to:
☑ Respect the guidelines for flexibility development and safety
☑ Ensure that all participants are challenged appropriately
☑ Ensure that all participants are continuously active
☑ Use teaching methods that will reach visual, auditory and kinaesthetic learners.

WEEK 7 - Coach

Coaching Tasks
❑ Discuss your warm-up and cool-down activities with your supervisor coach.
❑ Discuss how you will assist your coach during the rest of the lesson.
❑ Lead the entire warm-up and cool-down portions of the lesson.
❑ Assist where required.

WEEK 7 - Reflection

What worked well?_____

_____

How did the participants respond to your instructions? _____

_____

Did anything not go as planned? Why? How would you fix this problem?_____

_____

What would you change the next time you do these activities?_____

_____

_____

Discuss your reflections with your supervisor coach & note additional things that you need to remember:

_____

_____

WEEK 8 - Review What You Know

Motor Abilities

Complete the table to show that you understand the different motor abilities of agility, balance, coordination and spatial orientation. These 4 motor abilities are important for success in all gymnastics sports. Use your Gymnastics Foundations manual to complete the table.

	Definition	3 examples from my sport
Agility		
Balance		
Coordination		
Spatial orientation		

What is the difference between static balance and dynamic balance?

WEEK 8 - Learn Something New

Using Theme Days

Theme Days are great for adding variety, fun and excitement to your program. They can help to reinforce certain concepts or FMPs. They can entice participants to try new activities and they can stimulate the imagination and creativity of gymnasts and coaches alike.

Theme Days can be as simple or complicated as you like. You can inform parents the week before of special theme day (for example, pyjama day or teddy bear day) so that the participants arrive ready and eager to participate, or you can surprise the group by using different equipment or activities that carry a movement theme throughout the class. Regardless of your theme, plan carefully, and keep safety in mind at all times. Costumes or props should never interfere with movement, and participants should never be encouraged to take unnecessary risks.

Here are some ideas for themes, and some ways that they could be integrated with concepts in gymnastics. Remember that appropriate music is a great way to reinforce a theme. Use it in warm-ups, for games and even during circuits.

Special Holiday Themes - "Valentine's Day"	*Do partner skills and activities, gymnasts help each other with activities, play cooperative games, be friends with your group members, give out Valentines and wear red and white!*
Superhero Day	*Include activities that require great power and strength – lots of springing and locomotion activities. Find ways to move like different superheroes in various scary situations. And don't forget about "Elasti-girl"! Draw a mask around everyone's eyes for effect. (No capes!)*
Seasonal Themes - "Spring"	*Apart from the obvious, you can also include activities and skills that explore changes in level – e.g. growing from low to high – and changes in range (from small to large). A good theme for imagination games.*
Zoo or Jungle or Safari Day	*Great for animal walks, circuit set-ups (bars make a great jungle and you can train lions to jump through hoops) and imagination games. All FMPs fit well in this theme.*

Theme days can be handy for those times of the year when participants are cooped up in the house or school due to extreme cold or a spell of rainy weather. A few days of indoor recesses (or even a full moon!) will often provide you with a group of highly energetic participants, and parents who are grateful for an opportunity to see this energy expended in a positive manner. A dynamic Superhero theme day at these times of the year could be a useful trick to have in your back pocket.

Take a few minutes and write down some of your own ideas for Theme Days:

1. _____
2. _____
3. _____
4. _____
5. _____
6. _____
7. _____
8. _____
9. _____
10. _____

WEEK 8 – Create and Plan

Creating Theme Days

Pick your favourite Theme Day idea and design a warm-up, a game, two different 'apparatus' activities and a cool down activity that follow this theme. Describe each in detail, and identify the FMPs, the physical/motor abilities and/or specific skills that are being developed in each activity.

Theme:_____

*Warm-up – What are your participants developing?*_____

*Game – What are your participants developing?*_____

*Apparatus/Activity 1 – What are your participants developing?*_____

*Apparatus/Activity 2 – What are your participants developing?*_____

*Apparatus/Activity 3 – What are your participants developing?*_____

*Apparatus/Activity 4 – What are your participants developing?*_____

*Cool-down – What are your participants developing?*_____

WEEK 8 - Coach

Coaching Tasks

☐ Discuss your Theme Day activities with your supervisor coach.
☐ Discuss how you will assist your coach during the rest of the lesson.
☐ Lead at least 3 of your Theme Day activities during the lesson.
☐ Assist where required.

WEEK 8 - Reflection

*What worked well?*_____
_____

How did the participants respond to your instructions? _____
_____

*Did anything not go as planned? Why? How would you fix this problem?*_____
_____
_____

*What would you change the next time you do these activities?*_____
_____
_____

Discuss your reflections with your supervisor coach & note additional things that you need to remember:
_____
_____
_____

WEEK 9 – Review What You Know

Rotation

What causes a body to rotate?

_____

_____

_____

Name the 3 axes of rotation & list 2 skills in your sport for each. If your sport does not include skills that rotate around one of the axes, identify which axe of rotation is not used and why?

Axe of rotation	3 examples per axe or rotation from my sport

WEEK 9 – Learn Something New

Teaching process – organization and set-up

- ☝ Always thing about how to start and finish an activity.
- ☝ Always take into account the safety issues of the activity.
- ☝ Organize the activity so the participants are active for as long as possible.
- ☝ Set up the environment so you can move around and see everyone without interfering.
- ☝ Ensure that the participants get involved in the activity quickly (rapid transition)
- ☝ Ensure each participant has the maximum amount of practice time (number of repetitions).
- ☝ Always plan what equipment to use during the activity, prepare it ahead of time, and make sure it is available at the time of the activity.

Teaching process – explanations and demonstrations

👍 Always give participants cues or reference points (what they should look for or feel while doing the movement).

👍 Effective cues are short, clear, simple, and few (2 or 3).

👍 A cue must be observable by the coach and easily understood by the participant.

👍 Always show and tell the participant what successful performance will look and feel like (how will the participant know that he or she has succeeded).

👍 Be sure to use words, movements, or visuals that take into account the preferred learning styles of each participant (visual, auditory, kinesthetic, imagery).

👍 Make sure ALL the participants are positioned so they can hear and see.

👍 A good demonstration has the following characteristics: the movement is well executed, the timing is right, and everyone can see it.

👍 Consider using a participant as the demonstrator.

Teaching process – observation and feedback

👍 Always ensure participants understand the instructions you provided.

👍 Always ensure that the activity is appropriate for the participants' skill level.

👍 Always ensure that there is a good rate of success among the participants (i.e. most of the participants are able to do what you asked them to do).

👍 Actively supervise participants so you see ALL participants during the activity. Scanning the activity and moving around to watch what is going on from different vantage points enable you to be actively involved.

👍 Look to see if the participants are having fun, or if they are bored or discouraged.

👍 Pick up indications or signs of sound execution – or lack of it – and intervene quickly to correct the situation.

👍 Give feedback that is…

☑ Specific, not general, for example: "You did ___ perfectly" instead of "That's great!"

☑ Positive and constructive, not negative and humiliating

☑ Focus on behaviour that can be improved

☑ Informative and relevant

☑ Balanced – contains information on what the participant did well and what still needs improvement. For example, "Your ___ (movement) is better than last time. The next thing to do would be to (add another level of complexity to the movement, or a particular piece to refine.)".

☑ Clear, precise and easy to understand

Remember that a participant will need to spend many hours, weeks, months and even years to become a top notch performer. Your challenge as a coach will be to avoid long line-ups, inactivity and boring repetition. You must find creative ways to challenge your participants to improve while keeping them motivated to continue participating in sport.

WEEK 9 - Create and Plan

Design a circuit or series of activities to teach rotations using a variety of apparatus/aides:
- ☑ If designing a circuit, don't forget to count the number of participants in your group – you should have a minimum of 1 station per pair up to a maximum of 1 per participant.
- ☑ If designing activities, you must plan at least 6 different activities using at least 3 different 'apparatus'
- ☑ Don't forget to plan the best position for you to be in so you can observe all the participants.

Coaching Tasks

❑ Discuss your Rotation circuit / activities with your supervisor coach.

❑ Discuss how you will assist your coach during the rest of the lesson.

❑ Lead your Rotation circuit / activities during the lesson.

❑ Assist where required.

WEEK 9 - Reflection

*What worked well?*_____

_____

_____

How did the participants respond to your instructions? _____

_____

_____

*Did anything not go as planned? Why? How would you fix this problem?*_____

_____

_____

_____

*What would you change the next time you do this circuit/activities?*_____

_____

_____

_____

Discuss your reflections with your supervisor coach & note additional things that you need to remember:

_____

_____

_____

_____

_____

_____

_____

WEEK 10 - Review What You Know

Spring

Where can springs occur from?

What are the 3 mechanical conditions of good spring technique?

1. _____
2. _____
3. _____

WEEK 10 - Learn Something New

Qualities of Movement

Throughout the Gymnastics Foundations Introduction course we looked at ways to add variety in the program. In fact, any movement skill can be varied by manipulating the components of movement. You can create an infinite number of new skills, games and activities, simply by changing one or more components of movement. Below is a summary of general human movement, which you can use to help you in the exercise that follows.

What moves...		Where Movement takes place...				Qualities of movement...		
BODY		**SPACE**				**EFFORT**		
Body Part	Body Action	Ranges	Levels	Pathways	Direction	Time	Force	Rhythm
Arms	Stretched	Small	High	Straight	Forward	Fast/slow	Smooth	Move to
Legs	Bent	Medium	Medium	Curved	Backward	Long/short	Strong	the beat
Trunk	Twisted	Large	Low	Zigzag	Sideways	Accelerate	Gentle	of music
Feet	Crossed				Up	Decelerate	Explosive	
					Down		Heavy	
							light	

Now select a skill from the list below and find at least 6 ways to vary the performance of the skill. Use the box below to describe/draw your variations.

Skills (select one): forward roll, cartwheel, skipping, passé balance, 2-foot jump

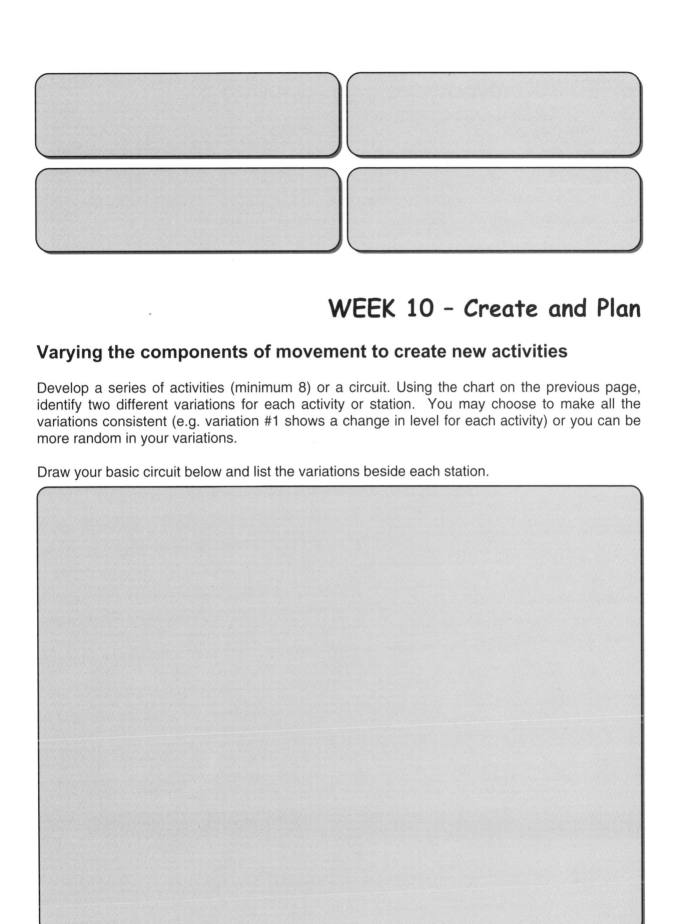

WEEK 10 - Create and Plan

Varying the components of movement to create new activities

Develop a series of activities (minimum 8) or a circuit. Using the chart on the previous page, identify two different variations for each activity or station. You may choose to make all the variations consistent (e.g. variation #1 shows a change in level for each activity) or you can be more random in your variations.

Draw your basic circuit below and list the variations beside each station.

WEEK 10 - Coach

Coaching Tasks

- ❑ Discuss your circuit / activities with your supervisor coach.
- ❑ Discuss how you will assist your coach during the rest of the lesson.
- ❑ Lead your circuit / activities during the lesson.
- ❑ Assist where required.

WEEK 10 - Reflection

*What worked well?*_____
_____
_____

How did the participants respond to your instructions? _____
_____
_____

*Did anything not go as planned? Why? How would you fix this problem?*_____
_____
_____

*What would you change the next time you do these activities?*_____
_____
_____

Discuss your reflections with your supervisor coach & note additional things that you need to remember:
_____
_____
_____
_____

Looking at the bigger picture

Your Gymnastics Foundations training & practical coaching experience has focused on planning specific components of a lesson. You have worked with a NCCP certified coach who has set the general direction for the program, and who has created the framework for the session or year.

Your lesson plans have fit within this bigger program plan.
Review the lesson plans that you and your supervisor have used over the past 10 weeks and the 'program plan'. Using the checklist below, check off where the various physical and motor abilities, Fundamental Movement Patterns, skills, apparatus and apparatus, etc. were included in each week's lesson plan. **Use a pencil!**

Program Component	Week										Comments
	1	2	3	4	5	6	7	8	9	10	
Physical Abilities											
• Flexibility											
• Power											
• Strength											
• Endurance											
Motor Abilities											
• Balance											
• Coordination											
• Spatial Orientation											
FMPs (Special focus)											
• Landings											
• Statics											
• Locomotions											
• Rotations											
• Springs											
Apparatus											
•											
•											
•											
•											
•											
•											
Special Days (list)											
•											
•											
•											

Based on the checklist, answer these questions:

Were all the FMPs covered during the session? If not, why?

_____

_____

Were all of your sport's apparatus used during the session? If not, why not?

_____

_____

Does your checklist show any relationship between the FMPs and physical/motor abilities?

_____

_____

Do you see any patterns in the plan? Describe them.

_____

_____

Do you have any other questions or observations? Note them here:

_____

_____

Now describe the gymnasts you worked with:

Gender: ❑ Female   ❑ Male   ❑ Male & Female

List the number of gymnasts in each age group:

Age: _____ Children: 6-7 years   Level(s):_____

_____ Children: 8-9 years   Level(s):_____

_____ Pre-Puberty: 10-11 years   Level(s):_____

_____ Puberty Stage 1: 12-15 years Level(s):_____

Within each age group, are there important differences in:

Height and Weight   yes ( )   no ( )

Skill Level   yes ( )   no ( )

Level of Experience   yes ( )   no ( )

Final assessment

You have now completed your practical coaching experience. How you feel about your experience and how you feel about your coaching capabilities? Complete the Coaching Self-Assessment questionnaire and the questions on the following page to find out.

COACH SELF-ASSESSMENT

On the form below, rate your level of confidence on a scale from 1 (low) to 5 (high).

How confident do you feel in your ability to:

	☹		☺		☺
Planning:	1	2	3	4	5
Plan warm-up and cool-down activities					
Plan gymnastics games					
Plan activities to develop physical abilities					
Plan activities to develop motor abilities					
Plan activities to develop the FMPs					
Plan circuit-type activities to maximize the time and space available					
Plan activities that are fun, challenging and safe, and ensure continuous activity					
Develop a lesson plan					
Teaching:	1	2	3	4	5
Teach warm-up and cool-down activities					
Teach gymnastics games					
Teach activities that develop physical and motor abilities					
Teach activities that develop the FMPs					
Teach circuits that are safe and which maximize the time and space available					
Teach activities that are fun, challenging and safe and ensure continuous activity					
Assess gymnasts' progress using CANGYM, CANJUMP, PRISM or other program					

Now turn the page, and answer the questions......

Did you enjoy this practical coaching experience? Why (or why not!)?

_____
_____
_____

What are your strongest skills as a coach?

_____
_____
_____

What areas of your coaching would you like to improve?

_____
_____
_____

In what aspects of coaching would you like more information or training?

_____
_____
_____

Discuss your reflections with your supervisor and note any additional comments that you need to remember:

_____
_____
_____
_____
_____
_____
_____

CONGRATULATIONS - You have completed the
Gymnastics Foundations Practical Coaching Component ☺
You may now register for the
Gymnastics Foundations Theory course!